Conflict Im... Project Management

"Some projects fail. Others succeed. This book is a must-read for those who want to succeed."
— LEN BIEGEL
Crisis Management Expert and author of *Never Say Never: The Complete Executive Guide to Crisis Management*

Praise for
"Are You a King or Queen of Conflict... in Project Management?"

"Are we the ruler of or a slave to conflict? If we allow ourselves to be a slave bowing to every conflict situation, we are putting our project and our careers in jeopardy. This book transforms us from a potential impotent slave to a decisive ruler; in other words, a king or queen of conflict. The key that opens this door to healthy conflict is Dave Gerber's and Dave Maurer's F.A.C.T.S. (Fear, Anger, Control, Trust, and Synergy) model which is mapped directly to each of the Project Management Institute's PMBOK nine Knowledge Areas. This book offers us practical, doable tools and techniques to deal with conflict situations. It is the only book that I am aware of on this topic that is specifically written for those of us in the project management discipline. This book is not about would-be's and should-be's, but is a guidebook to action and success as a project manager. Have your notepad or a highlighter with you when you read it. You'll want to capture ideas that you can use immediately. Wishing you an outstanding reading experience!"
— JOAN KNUTSON
Noted project manager, entrepreneur, keynote speaker and author. Recognized by PMI as one of the top 25 most influential women in project management.

Are You a
KING or QUEEN
of CONFLICT...
in Project Management?

BY DAVE GERBER AND DAVE MAURER

Published by Timeless Publishing

www.timelesspublishing.com

info@timelesspublishing.com

ISBN: 978-0-9788707-2-0

Library of Congress Control Number: 2008903874

Series I

Printed in the United States of America

Special thanks for our cover layout to Jeff Calabria
and production support to Robert Allan & Associates.

Special thanks to Gaye Newton, Kris Munster and Tina Maurer
for their high quality editing and thoughtful suggestions.

More Praise for
"Are You a King or Queen of Conflict...
in Project Management?"

"Dave Gerber and Dave Maurer have offered a unique and interesting perspective on the relationship between the tenets of project management and the inevitability of conflict. The cross-referencing of the nine knowledge areas of the PMBOK and the insightful F.A.C.T.S. model, used to describe the impact of conflict on our work, adds significantly to our project management literature. This book will prove its usefulness to any project manager or team leader interested in working through conflict to get the job done."

— RON TAYLOR
> Project manager, lecturer, trainer, author, and consultant, and the principal and founder of the Ron Taylor Group.

"Conflict is ever present in the securities markets since each transaction has a buyer with one set of beliefs and a seller with an opposite position. I wish I had this set of tools as I tried to navigate conflict as a senior executive of a Wall Street firm. This book practically and powerfully teaches the reader how to use many tools, including how to apply 20 points of success to transform conflict into a creative process that bridges the differences between parties and results in collaborative agreements. Following the F.A.C.T.S. process will allow any project manager or team member to mitigate differing opinions and keep projects on time, within budget and on course...highly recommended for converting conflict into a positive, creative and successful set of results."

— GLENN FAULKNER
> Former senior officer and executive of the NASDAQ Stock Market, Co-Founder of Innovative Negotiations

Acknowledgements

*"As we express our gratitude, we must never forget that
the highest appreciation is not to utter words, but to live by them."*
– JFK

I would like to acknowledge a great colleague and friend Dave Maurer, for his continual support and work together on many projects, including this one. I would like to thank my wife, Kakki, my daughter, Jessie, my parents, my brother and all of those who have helped me to build a wonderful business and life of helping others. I would also like to thank Alice McDowell, a college professor, who helped me fundamentally change the way I view the world and my life-long project of self improvement. Thank you. – DAVE GERBER

My heartfelt thanks to my wife, Tina, for her love, patience and guidance. For 30 years, she has been my inspiration and my light. To my late father, my unending gratitude for teaching me about leadership by his stellar example. My thanks to my mother, who continues to teach me the importance of compassion, and is the reason I am who I am. All the blemishes are my own. Finally, to my wonderful sons, Dan, Brian and Chris—all fine young men with bright futures and unlimited potential. I could not be more proud of their service to others and our nation.

Working with Dave and learning more about the tenets of conflict management only added to my desire to explore all of this and share what I found. Many of the ideas and concepts included in this book have been on my mind for 20 years – since about the time I really started to appreciate what leadership really is all about. In the private sector, and more specifically, working in the field of project management, I found that many of the leadership and management principles practiced in the military are directly transferable into the corporate world and nearly all facets of the modern workplace. – DAVE MAURER

Table of Contents

Foreword

Throughout history a special breed of men and women has been called upon by their peers to shoulder a unique responsibility. These exceptional individuals have left their mark on history, on society, and sometimes on geography; their combined efforts have molded our world.

Examples of their prowess include the Egyptian Pyramids, the Great Wall of China and the great medieval cathedrals of Europe; these and other achievements stand as testament to their skill in harnessing and coordinating the efforts of mankind in order to achieve greatness. We often read of their accomplishments as if the buildings, the transportation systems, the ships or the siege machines materialized from thin air. The fact is, nothing ever materializes from thin air.

Read history carefully and one can see beyond the names of the great kings and the conquering generals into the very heart of greatness, down to the extraordinary individuals who have possessed the skills and intellect to make great things happen. These individuals, whose names have often been lost to history, were the pioneers in what today we call Project Management.

For example, the Spartans at Thermopylae, led by their king Leonidas, still serve today as the finest example of bravery and sacrifice. Less understood are the individuals who produced the standardized weapons with which the Spartans fought and which enabled the phalanx to succeed as a warfighting formation, who achieved the manufacture of the armor which so successfully protected the hoplite warriors, who efficiently collected and transported the food and water which sustained the Spartan Army in the field, and who ultimately buried the soldiers and then immortalized them.

When viewed in this historic framework the challenge of "Project Management" may sound prosaic. Far from it. It is precisely Project Management which unleashes that unique set of skills which enables mankind to achieve greatness. In this wide-ranging book Dave Gerber and Dave Maurer skillfully take on the task of capturing the breadth of this special skill set and communicating that skill set to the reader.

Based squarely upon the Guide to the Project Management Body Of Knowledge (PMBOK) promulgated by the industry-leading Project Management Institute, the authors provide a thorough review of the many theories and methodologies which educate and inspire the modern Project Manager.

You can't beat this book when it comes to learning and understanding Project Management and the concepts, the perceptions and the accumulated learning of centuries which has so revolutionized successful project achievement over the past few decades.

– WALKER LEE EVEY
President and CEO
Design-Build Institute of America
Program Manager, Pentagon Renovation
Program and Project Phoenix: Rebuilding
the Damaged Pentagon Following the
Attacks of 911; Former Senior Advisor
to the Iraqi Ministry of Housing

Are You a
KING or QUEEN
of CONFLICT...
in Project Management?
BY DAVE GERBER AND DAVE MAURER

Preface

Why Read this Book?

Sometimes fear gets the best of us. As project managers we can often feel that we can take on the entire project single-handedly, and do a better and faster job than if we had to deal with all the personalities and agendas (both overt and hidden) that are inherent in leading a team. If any endeavor in the world of work is ripe for issues of conflict, it's project management!

There must be thousands of definitions and interpretations of project management. Some are cultural, some are unique to certain business units and fields of endeavor, some are free wheeling and open to interpretation, and still more are very precise and not subject to ambiguity.

In its simplest terms, a project:
- is going from nothing to something
- has a specific and measurable timeframe
- has a beginning, a middle and an end
- has a desired outcome
- has unique characteristics
- is time-phased and milestone-driven
- follows a repeatable, yet flexible process

Projects appear everywhere around us. Think about the size of the undertakings when completing projects such as rebuilding the World Trade Center or the reconstruction of huge sections of the Pentagon. The "Big Dig" subway system in Boston is one, the individual space shuttle missions are others. On a less grand scale, construction of a new bridge or overpass offer glimpses into the world of project management as does the planning and conduct of a large event, such as the New York City Marathon. Projects are discrete events, and more to our purpose in this book, they are planned, overseen and concluded by a project manager with the help of others.

No single person builds a house, let alone launches the space shuttle. It takes a team and, therefore, teamwork to bring any large project to fruition. Teamwork brings us back to the world of conflict—as the two are rarely separated by more than a moment. Those teams need a leader, a project manager!

"There is nothing more difficult to take in hand,
more perilous to conduct, or more uncertain in its success,
than to take the lead in the introduction of a new order of things."
– NICCOLO MACHIAVELLI

I.
Essential Project Management Conflict Questions

"This feeling, finally, that we may change things –
this is at the centre of everything we are.
Lose that…lose everything."
– SIR DAVID HARE

When we take the time to slow down, listen and learn, we often find that our desire to seek grows stronger than our fear of being wrong. The following are 13 Essential Questions that will get to the heart of conflict-related issues. These are the stake in the ground for our exploration throughout this text. To that end, further answers to these questions will be explored in greater detail and from different perspectives.

1. What is Conflict?

Most project managers know conflict when they sense it; many intuitively understand what is about to happen and work to create resolution before it has even happened. Whether it is individuals who disagree on results, process, needs, values or underlying interests, conflict happens in many ways, all of the time.

The following comprehensive list of conflict definitions was compiled by Gregg Walker, Professor of Speech Communication at Oregon State University. We think familiarity with a number of definitions helps to create more clarity and fluency around the subject.

"Social conflict is a struggle between opponents over values and claims to scarce status, power and resources."

"Conflicts that are strategic are essentially bargaining situations in which the ability of one participant to gain his ends is dependent on the choices or decisions that the other participant will make."

"A conflict exists whenever incompatible activities occur . . . one party is interfering, disrupting, obstructing, or in some other way making another party's actions less effective."

"Conflict is a process in which two or more parties attempt to frustrate the other's goal attainment . . . the factors underlying conflict are threefold: interdependence, differences in goals, and differences in perceptions."

"Conflict means perceived divergence of interest, or a belief that the parties' current aspirations cannot be achieved simultaneously."

"Conflicts are communicative interactions among people who are interdependent and who perceive that their interests are incompatible, inconsistent, or in tension."

"Conflict is the interaction of interdependent people who perceive incompatible goals and interference from each other in achieving those goals."[1]

Regardless of which definition(s) we identify with, it is clear that many people choose to engage in or escalate conflict, rather than move slowly and make decisions based on the outcomes they want. Some people can even become "emotionally hijacked," a changing physiological state where blood pressure increases and chemicals are released in the brain causing us to feel differently.

When you have a panic attack, or become very anxious, your emotional response can actually bypass your 'thinking brain.' The…amygdale [small but powerful part of the brain], which is involved with creating a 'faster than thought' panic attack… [gets triggered]. It is very difficult, or impossible, to think clearly when highly emotional because the part of the brain you think with is inhibited…This response has been termed an "emotional hijacking" by Daniel Goleman.[2]

Our brains are hardwired, unfortunately in some instances, in a primitive way designed to protect ourselves. While there are no more saber-tooth tigers threatening us today, conflict stimulates our programmed, primitive response in a similar way it did thousands of years ago. As in our past, some current situations ignite those reflexive body and mind changes that we seem to have to work very hard to control, if control is even possible.

Whether conflict manifests itself in an immediate, in-our-face situation or during an ongoing relationship within a set of variables inside a project or the project itself, it affects *who* we are—the very core of our being, the person we speak to when we talk to ourselves. Conflict may be triggered when we believe our needs and values are in question or in jeopardy of being met. This can result in frustration and can make us cynical. Not surprisingly, too much of our self talk is negative.

Conflict often happens when obstacles appear, when we fixate on our pre-determined outcomes instead of our underlying needs. Conflict surfaces when we lack the desire to comprehend what others are saying before we attempt to be understood, when we believe that *our* perception is the only one, and when we do not listen actively. Such conflicts, within a project or not, are usually based on our issues and ability to deal effectively with fear, anger, control, or a lack of synergy or trust.

All project managers are subject to this phenomenon, especially the strongest and most experienced project managers. Why? Because the more we know (or think we know) about the task or mission at hand, the less likely we are to be very receptive to an alternate view or approach and shift from our default behavior.

2. Is the conflict that Project Managers face positive or negative?

The likelihood of conflict in a project setting with multiple team members is 100%! If we don't acknowledge that some degree of conflict in inevitable, we have probably never been on a team, or we were just not paying enough attention to our teammates or surroundings.

Actually, conflict is not always a bad thing; it can be both positive and negative. As we alluded earlier, conflict can do a number of things. Confrontation driven by positive conflict will often be the only way to proactively deal with issues that people or groups need to address. Conflict can be the beginning of any great thing or the ending of something that needs closure.

Positive conflict **can:**
- Be the start to something new
- Initiate change
- Reinforce leadership ranks when appropriate
- Energize the team to think "outside the box"
- Disintegrate leadership distinction when appropriate
- Improve time management or resource control
- Positively redirect something that was off track
- Promote understanding of competing perspectives
- Support dialogue
- Align personal objectives with team objectives
- Enlighten someone who is unaware of a problem
- Uncover unforeseen possible solutions and outcomes
- Create closure
- Be the start of something unexpected
- Become a life-long learning opportunity
- Foster self-esteem, trust, motivation, loyalty and teamwork
- Encourage top-notch performance
- Reinforce our current abilities, strengths or contributions
- Help work toward team "happiness" and "high performance"

But remember, just because it is positive does not mean that it will necessarily be easy or painless.

Negative conflict **can:**
- Create more or unnecessary conflict
- Create impediments to honesty and trust
- Create physiological responses that impede our ability to make sound, cognitive, logical decisions
- Sabotage decision making
- Undermine innovation
- Disintegrate timelines and results
- Re-emphasize past poor decision making
- Trigger our default behavior that creates more conflict
- Reduce communication
- Shut down cooperation and participation
- Hinder information flow
- Cripple critical thinking and limit analysis
- Eliminate effective brainstorming
- Limit commitment to the process and the product
- Expose hidden agendas
- Shift control to the wrong person
- Increase cost through inefficiency
- Damage thorough planning
- Create destructive alliances
- Cause anxiety, mental and physical stress and/or sickness
- Annihilate respect and trust among teammates
- Impede our ability to collectively attain our goals
- Impede professional development
- Create and sustain team wars
- Promote inter-departmental silos

As previously mentioned, positive conflict, by its very nature, can signal a moment to explore perspectives, look at common interests, open lines of communication, generate learning opportunities and help us to separate the people from the problem.

Far too often, people react to conflict negatively with anger, avoidance, fear, poor communication techniques or an absolute shutdown. But it is equally possible for individuals to choose positive thinking, to brainstorm and to produce new perspectives, ideas and even a new road map or new dynamic. The process can strengthen character and reinforce how we view and ultimately use conflict to our advantage. Anything less can force the conflict to remain below the surface.

It is this undercurrent of unresolved conflict that poses the most danger. It really is like that covered pot of boiling water that, left unattended, can cause an explosion. It is the job of the team leader or project manager to look for these possible problems, confront them early, openly and often and hence, turn down the heat. If we as project managers are happily and nonchalantly flying through our tasks and missions, we may be in denial!

3. Resource constraints are expected. What can we do to mitigate their effects and the conflict that can result?

The temptation at the outset of any project is to assume we will enjoy the use of every available dollar, every staff member initially assigned, and all the technology required to be at our beck and call. That expectation fades after a few hours (maybe minutes) and the new reality of living and working with less than we wanted sets in. This is when the prepared project manager asks him/herself and those on the team the key question: What do we need to complete this project? Even then, some of what we deemed essential will evaporate. Competing requirements, other critical projects, more demanding project managers and a thousand other reasons can drain the resources we thought were ours. There should be no surprise that these conditions will produce opportunities to experience conflict - a great deal of conflict!

It becomes vital to the success of the project that the project leader demonstrate the capability to operate in a "constraint-rich" environment. Prioritization of tasks and deliverables is crucial at this time. Doing more (or even the expected) with less can be daunting, so a keen awareness of what is important and what isn't can go a long way to stabilizing the team and the project. Further, keying in on task management, schedules, and integration efforts will help mitigate the effects of a less than optimal working environment.

Think of all the great accomplishments throughout history, and we will undoubtedly discover that each one occurred under similar conditions of scarcity. Let's imagine the problems faced by the appointed project manager for Stonehenge, the prehistoric monument located on the Salisbury Plains of England. Begun in 3100 BC and continuing into 2200 BC, the series of project managers over those many years must have shared the same concerns of the very first. "You want me to build what? Where? With what?" Though they were all likely not short on some resources (time and manpower), they absolutely had to deal with the fact that the bluestones used in the construction were not found within 200 miles of the construction site.

Finding the right material, transporting it to the site and then devising the means to erect the huge pieces in place have been the subject of hundreds of books and documentaries. It's the very fact that this was "difficult" that makes it special. The constraints that existed then exist now in any number of modern projects, great and small.

The point is that the project managers and those in control of resources found a way to overcome tremendous shortages and still accomplish the mission. There is a lesson here for all of us. Ask questions, find out exactly what is expected, consider all possible options and solutions, decide on the best course of action, prioritize tasks, and then ACT.

4. Our most significant and volatile resources are the people with whom we work—our team leaders, teammates and stakeholders. How does conflict impact our optimization of human resources?

It is true that the very people we must have available to accomplish the work, are quite often our most fleeting resource. Unlike materials and other resources, people do have a mind of their own and can choose to abandon a project or project team at any moment. We can start the project fully staffed, but attrition is a fact that all managers have encountered over time.

With attrition comes the inevitable cost of a gapped or vacant position for some period, extra work for those remaining, the search process, and the inherent challenges of finding the best fit for the job (personality, record, competency, etc.), and then infusion into the team. Multiply this by the number of typical personnel changes and we quickly see that the management of human resources is a necessary one to master. The project manager is ultimately responsible for the smooth running of the project team. This is rarely an easy task, yet it's often the one that determines ultimate success.

5. Given that successful project management is largely dependent upon process, how can we create efficient and effective processes to facilitate mission accomplishment and smooth the effects of conflict?

We have stated elsewhere in this book that project management is a time-phased, milestone-driven, repeatable *process*. It certainly is that and much more, to be sure, especially when individuals focus on process as it pertains to both managing and leading projects and dealing with the effects of conflict.

First, it should be our goal to use process to reduce conflict by minimizing confusion, distraction and turbulence caused by unclear instructions, bewildering direction and inconsistent decisions. Process can be the rudder needed to steer the project "ship" toward the objective. Problems arise when the process chosen is so inflexible that it becomes an obstacle.

Processes can be both dependably familiar and reliable while being responsive to change. Our established processes must be designed to work *for* us, thus they need to be as accommodating as necessary to serve the project manager during times of turmoil and uncertainty. When crafting processes or adapting existing processes and procedures to meet our needs, we must be thinking outside the box and looking for long-term solutions that will stand the test of time.

During the life cycle of a given project, turnover will occur, some key positions will transition—all this while targets move, scope changes and heretofore unyielding requirements are summarily "adjusted." A well thought out process model can save us and the project, even during the most volatile phases of the endeavor.

6. How does truth telling impact Project Managers?

We have included this as an Essential Question because we believe it is important to take responsibility for the results of our actions. Presenting false impressions can be a source of conflict. For some, it can become an endless river of fuel, feeding flames of conflict, draining the parties involved for years or even decades. It is not unlike flammable peat moss burning below the surface of the earth, waiting to break through and create a massive fire. It takes new lies to keep the old lies fresh. The importance of honesty is addressed again further in this book.

What is a lie? A lie can be defined as presenting any other paradigm, regardless of how minimal the difference, than the one we believe to be true. How is information deleted, removed, or reorganized to change the paradigm? How are elements of time manipulated? While there are many ways to manipulate the truth, it is also important to investigate what our parents and extended family socialized us to believe is the truth.[3]

People have always wondered why people lie. We often fear being judged or being put in a position where we have to justify our decisions, behaviors and comments. Certainly, project leaders of all stripes will report that the opportunity to "fabricate a bit" presents itself quite often in the life cycle of a project. The truth, to be sure, can hurt (usually the project manager) and cause grief among the stakeholders and project sponsors.

Opportunities to alter the truth or simply lie about the facts tend to occur around some of the basic interest areas of project sponsors and leaders. Questions about budget variances, schedules, key integration points and quality may tempt even the best project manager or team member to misrepresent the truth. Of course, these lies don't hold up for long and the negative results of the lie will usually far outweigh the original problem. Our credibility is forever damaged and rightly so. Our integrity will be questioned in every instance, big or small, once we demonstrate the willingness to offer an easy lie rather than the hard truth.

Does truth mean the entire story? If details, insignificant or not, are left out, has a lie been told? When considering the definition of a lie in the project management world, determine whether our team members and other project leaders define it similarly. If not, why not? How does each person's understanding of truth impact the amount of conflict they create for themselves and others?

So why else do project managers and team members lie? Perhaps to reduce conflict, being judged or evaluated. Lies are told in this context to cover up resource issues and time management problems, not to mention the interpersonal issues. This may be done to ensure our leadership style will dominate, to keep people at a distance from the "truth," or to manipulate some of the variables—including people.

As project leaders, we want to move forward, reduce conflict so we don't slow progress and get mired in endless debate. The motivation to lie in this instance appears solid and can easily be rationalized as necessary for the greater good, whatever that might be at the moment. Of course, the opportunity to lie and the means and motivation to do so are found at nearly every turn while working on a project. Leaders may lie to project team members or withhold information. Project sponsors may not get the entire picture at every briefing, and team members may not be sharing the truth at the 100% level every time they speak.

Truth telling during the creation and implementation of projects is truly about the types of choices we make around honesty. And, there are always consequences. Even if we do not want to be judged or have to justify our legitimate feelings to each other, we still make a choice when asked to tell the truth or when we are expected to fill in the details.

7. Why should Project Managers understand the difference between positions and interests?

Understanding and using interest-based conflict management styles in our lives will allow us to move beyond difficult situations with others.

In typical project management settings where some degree of conflict is almost inevitable, the possibility of somehow achieving a win-win solution is enticing to all concerned parties. In a team environment—as found in many project-driven settings—agreeing on the way ahead (the planning stage) can present the most difficult challenges of the project. This is why we generally spend what appears to be an inordinate percentage of time in the planning phase as opposed to the execution or controlling phases.

How can that be? Certainly, we know that poor planning can result in lousy execution. History is replete with examples in the military, politics and business. But it's not just that we spend more time planning so we can get it right; we spend more time planning because its is HARD to do. We will discuss this more in subsequent sections.

We believe this is one of the most important elements for individuals to capture as they move through this book. People often stick to their pre-determined outcomes because they are angry, hurt, or feeling unheard. Yet these emotions get in the way of win-win solutions.

When two people enter into conflict focused on resolution that satisfies only their pre-determined outcome, they tend to resort to protecting their positions, feelings and thoughts. When those involved can focus on criteria that meets the underlying needs of both parties, the solution will be more acceptable—the elusive win-win.

Think of the question, "What do you need?" This is a much more forward-thinking approach. Focusing on interests allows us to concentrate on why a particular solution is preferred. It generates explanations, not justification, and promotes progress toward a customized, designed, longer lasting and clarified win-win solution.

8. What is the role of preparation when dealing with conflict situations?

There are times in the life of a project that it may seem as if planning doesn't matter. As mentioned earlier, we can plan for weeks, consuming the bulk of most project timelines, but once the first meeting occurs, or the first major decision is made, we often find the need to adjust and move to "Plan B" or even further down the contingency ladder, perhaps to a point where there may be no pre-conceived plan at all.

For example, in the military it is said that all plans are fine right up until the first shot is fired. With lives and sometimes the fate of nations at stake, the military can't just accept this and drive on. Military planners have mastered the art of contingency planning and negotiating fluid operations. This contingency planning also serves to reduce conflict down the road among and between the various interested parties. We can and must do the same in the work of project management. If we expect the unexpected, we will not be surprised or disappointed.

In order to prevent those types of feelings, planning for difficult discussions, negotiations, performance assessment or team issues, the Synergy Planning Guide can help create more, well-planned thinking that leads to better outcomes (see Appendix, page 83.)

9. What are the differences between conflict prevention, management and resolution? [4]

Government in our country—and others too, for that matter—now resonates with "Crisis Response Teams" or some similar entity. They exist in just about every level of government from federal to state, county and local, all designed to deal with the aftermath of a particular crisis event.

Certainly our quick and appropriate response to crises is critical to the health and welfare of all concerned. We cannot predict every contingency, possible system failure, or every natural or manmade catastrophe. But we are now paying greater attention to *prevention* while building and maintaining an effective response mechanism. Prevention saves time, money and in some cases, lives and property.

Conflict prevention provides similar value. Managers and leaders at all levels are, in all likelihood, better served by anticipating, and then taking steps to prevent conflict, rather than having to manage it. Ironically, however, this is not a universal truth. Conflict, or better stated, *managed* conflict, can trigger and even promote improved teamwork and generate better decisions. Project leaders play the central role in how the team deals with conflict and everyone will be watching how the leader handles this responsibility. When we can control our reactions, allow the necessary time to think through the problem, and consider possible consequences, we are transforming our *reactions* into *responses*.

In a typical project setting, particularly when the stakes may be high but the risks are low, we tend to slant our planning more toward reaction and crisis management than toward prevention of the original crisis event. The investment in prevention (risk prevention) can be considerable and the return on investment may be too low or too unpredictable to support the investment cost. As our parents probably taught most of us, "an ounce of prevention is worth a pound of cure." This old axiom stands the test of time in just about every endeavor, and it is especially true for those of us practicing project management.

Taking the time, energy, resources and, quite often, money to prevent conflict before it starts is the only way to ensure that we are as prepared as we can be when conflict rears its head. When it does (and it will), we have to be prepared to understand the elements of conflict, its sources and its value when properly managed.

As described in *Use Conflict*, Human Beings = Conflict.[5] If we believe that premise, we can believe that preventing conflict is smart and rational and will positively affect our professional and personal lives. Whoever said that business wasn't personal wasn't looking beyond his or her experience on the project.

Conflict Prevention incorporates a wide range of thoughts, planning, behaviors and follow-up that creates informal and formal policies, procedures and practices.

Think about it. Would it be acceptable for a school to have a fire policy but only practice it every other year? No. Policies and procedures must be put to the test and practiced. The goal is to avert the problem or at least reduce the escalation and/or damage involved.

Conflict prevention **includes:**
1. Engaging in self-assessment, monitoring, and positive self-talk that will allow us to avert or manage a potentially disruptive conflict. Self-talk is widely viewed as the mini-internal discussions we have with ourselves, about our lives, during quiet times.
2. Understanding the Agents of Socialization and other root causes directly related to the conflict at hand, project conflict and others that play out in our life.
3. Understanding our own "hot buttons" or default behaviors enough to warn ourselves of an impending conflict and/or a potentially harmful reaction when leading projects or acting as a team member.
4. Developing a prevention-oriented mindset that understands, anticipates and proactively considers the impact of conflict in each area of personal and professional life; also, taking the steps to ensure it does not negatively impact our project or our team at any level.
5. Ensuring ourselves and those around us that we are dedicated to strengthening our interpersonal skills and preventing conflict in every aspect of life. Each project is another opportunity to learn, grow and do better the next time.

Conflict prevention addresses a desire to gain tools and skills that will help to ensure that negativity, or excessive and damaging conflict, never happens. But this new learning is only made useful when it is applied fairly and consistently with great reflection.

Conflict Management is about using conflict prevention and a mitigation mentality and working toward resolution, self-awareness and a system or procedure for immediately dealing with conflict. Project managers are constantly in a state of conflict management. Project management is a cyclical process of identifying, then extinguishing the conflicts that happen between people, and among resources.

Our goal is to prevent the initiation of conflict, quickly facilitate a method for containment when it happens and enable ourselves to transform the experience into solutions, calmness, growth and life-long learning.

Conflict resolution is a method or process of eliminating or handling a conflict, preferably quickly, by:
- Identifying the main, secondary, tertiary and related issues
- Addressing each side's (or internal competing) needs
- Adequately addressing personal and professional interests
- Investigating unmet professional expectations
- Understanding and anticipating the possible consequences of any decision (cause and effect)
- Allowing for the customized design of solutions between the parties involved in conflict
- Including all appropriate individuals and stakeholders
- Remaining solution oriented
- Creating a plan, making choices and confirming the outcomes
- Developing and following a plan that demands honest, effective feedback
- Actively listening to all parties involved, without interruption
- Resolving issues through arbitration, mediation, negotiation, alternative dispute resolution or a court of law

Though all of these steps were first listed in *"Use Conflict: Advance Your Winning Life"* by Dave Gerber, they read like a laundry list of "Dos" for the project leader. Chief among these and actually woven throughout nearly all of them is the notion of establishing and agreeing upon expectations.

It follows that the more we focus on conflict prevention, the less conflict we will have to manage and resolve. Each of these stages is a part of the process of transforming conflict into an agent for positive change. For instance, the identification and elimination of the conditions that fuel conflict and support prevention are crucial. Management is appropriate when conflict, as positive change, is critical for achieving the desired results. Resolution encompasses prevention and management, resulting in a paradigm shift toward win-win solutions for all parties involved.

Remember a time when we did not experience conflict? If we are honest with ourselves, the answer is usually no. From the beginning of our lives, screaming and crying was our only way to tell everyone that something in our world wasn't right. We were in conflict with our dirty diaper, a hungry belly, lack of warmth or attention, and sometimes pain. Conflict is a human phenomenon, a part of both the nature and nurture cycles.[6]

10. What are the Project Management basic skills I should learn and master to avoid basic conflicts?

Familiarity with or knowledge in the following areas of interest within the discipline of Project Management are important to achieving success as a project manager:

- Identification and definition of a project
- Development of specified and implied requirements
- Development of specified and implied tasks
- Work Breakdown Structures (WBS)
- Earned Value Management (EVM)
- Development of milestones and timelines
- Development of integrated schedules
- Network Diagrams
- Critical Path Method (CPM)
- Program Evaluation and Review Techniques (PERT)
- Activity sequencing
- Progress tracking
- Project management tools (Gantt charts, software, formulas, templates, etc.)
- Team development
- Team building
- Stakeholder management
- Conflict management and resolution
- Cost estimating/planning
- Managing to a budget
- Role of the team leader or project manager
- Role of the team member
- Anticipating and managing change
- Dealing with uncertainty

- Dealing with unpredictability
- Risk identification and management
- Procurement document types (types of contracts)
- Development and use of a Lessons Learned database
- Core Documents (Project Charters, Mission Need Statements, Project Management Plans, Quality Control Plans, etc.)
- **The 5 Process Groups** of a project (Initiating, Planning, Executing, Controlling and Closing)
- **The 9 Knowledge Areas** of project management (IAW the Project Management Body of Knowledge…Integration, Scope, Time, Cost, Quality, Human Resources, Communications, Risk, and Procurement)
- *Conflict fluency related to the 5 phases and 9 Knowledge Areas*

Anyone in nearly any position can conceivably be called upon to be a project team member or even lead a project. Therefore, all professionals should be exposed to the principles and tenets of project management as it is used in industry and government. Without a fundamental understanding of the above listed concepts, project managers are bound to run into basic conflicts that could be avoided and have a better understanding of how to comprehensively address larger conflict issues.

11. How will my understanding and implementation of the 5 Process Groups of a Project help me effectively deal with conflict and ultimately succeed?

The five "phases" of the project, or the Project Management Process Groups as espoused in the PMBOK Guide, represent the cornerstone of sound project management. They guide the user through the logical steps necessary to establish the need for the project, identify objectives, plan the approach, establish milestones and metrics, work the plan, adjust for change and end the project when appropriate. Though this sounds straight forward enough, there are sufficient variables and unplanned events that can significantly impede performance.

The five Process Groups are sequential, yet can and usually do overlap. They are again 1) Initiating, 2) Planning, 3) Executing, 4) Controlling and 5) Closing.[7]

As one might imagine, each offers opportunities to encounter conflict. Virtually no project is immune to the emergence of conflict situations or the effects of that conflict on the people involved and the project itself.

Conflict is even likely to become apparent as early as the Initiation Phase with the development of the Project Charter. Almost certainly, the terms and expectations of the project will differ from project sponsor to project team member and stakeholder. The project manager will not only have his or her own ideas about the project, but must now manage the infusion of disparate ideas into a coherent scope statement and clear charter language. The conflict opportunities continue to mount into the Planning Phase where they will probably deepen.

As was stated earlier, the Planning Phase often consumes the lion's share of the time given most projects. This phase, encompassing everything from issues of scope and quality to risk, cost and staffing, among others, is where project success is normally determined. Poor planning rarely yields acceptable results, so the work involved here, combined with the varying interests at play and the nature of our work in teams, sets the stage for a kind of "conflict conscientiousness."

As we move through planning and into the Executing and Controlling Phases, we are applying previously agreed upon standards and processes to our project and will again come face to face with differences of opinion and view of the way ahead. Finally, as we move into and through the Closing Phase, we are faced with adherence to established exit criteria, the unwilling-ness of some stakeholders, in many cases, to even close the project at all, and the process to end on time and within the budget.

The process of managing a project, complex or simple, is rife with conflict. The successful project manager anticipates this, is prepared for it and is willing to take the steps necessary to work through, with and beyond the obstacles that conflict presents. This requires the leader (be they the named leader of the project or those who exude a leadership presence within the project team), to find the best approach to conflict management given the circumstances at hand.

The search for the "win-win," integrated, and more permanent solution should drive our process. Within the parlance of the PMBOK Guide, this is in step with the "problem solving" conflict mode, more so than any other approach to dealing with conflict. Compromise brings some mutual success, but this integrated approach is both constructive and longer-lasting.

12. How can we identify potential problems based on conflict, address them by applying useful tools, and then obtain the outcome we desire?

One of the best concepts found in the PMBOK Guide is one of the simplest. The framework of using Inputs, Tools and Techniques and Outputs to move from start to finish is both clear and useful. We offer a variation on that theme using the same model for identifying problems (Inputs), methods to address them (Tools and Techniques) and achieving desired results (Outputs).

Juxtaposed against the F.A.C.T.S. model (see page 33), this creates a matrix and a unique and useful way to view the principal factors of conflict in following an accepted project management approach.

The problems and challenges for the project manager that arise from Fear, Anger, Control, Trust and Synergy issues are many and varied, which we will discuss as the central themes to this book.

Fear, what Dorothy Thompson called "the most destructive element in the human mind," manifests itself in a number of ways (*Inputs*). We fear insecurity, our own inexperience, and perhaps even our own incompetence or ignorance in a specific area. We fear a lack of "top cover" when we make a mistake and we may even fear success! By asking questions, learning as we perform, adjusting as needed, seeking the counsel of those around us and managing our emotional reaction to our fears, (*Tools and Techniques*), we can create the positive results we want and need. These results, (*Outputs*), include new confidence, independence, improved self-image, some level of expertise, and a more rational thinker.

Anger stemming from past offenses, long held grudges, frustration, immaturity or some other pain are all *inputs* that can be addressed with proper tools and techniques. Personal growth, learning to forgive and forget while accepting our own failures, can hasten our achievement of the desired output. Applied properly, these *techniques* can lead to a calmer, cooler and more relaxed version of ourselves. We will think more clearly, improve our ability to reason and "lengthen our fuse" so we are slower to anger in the future.

Typical *Control* issues plague us in several ways. Our relative position on the organization chart, our age (too young or too old) our time with the organization itself, and our apparent inability to influence leaders, open us to more opportunities to have to face conflict head on. Often, control issues are overcome with time. As we grow into the job, our influence widens and our credibility increases. We will build relationships, expand our network, and become better communicators with experience. The *outputs* we will then enjoy include the ability (and willingness) to accept more risk, work more efficiently and be more trusting while focusing on the needs of those around us.

The lack of *Trust* is manifested in even more obvious ways. These *inputs* might be low self-esteem, operating based on fear, hoarding information, working alone when teamwork is clearly optimal and an unwillingness to take others into one's confidence or inner circle. To overcome these obstacles, we must learn to delegate and accept the risk of the failure of others. This requires that we take the time to train, coach and mentor as necessary. The *outputs* we hope to realize include an exponentially increased presence in the enterprise – because we have "extended our reach" by building trusting relationships with others.

Finally, problems caused by the absence of *Synergy*, especially within the structure of project teams, will bring unwanted and often unforeseen problems. Poor integration, inadequate processes and procedures, stove-piping, poor collaboration, and even a substandard cross-training policy can lead to synergistic nightmares. We can apply training, team building exercises, and a more appropriate structure and organization. Synergy brings about efficiency and "smoothness" to work flow that is difficult to describe but understood by most managers. Accountability is properly distributed, the chain of supervision is made clear and conflict is dealt with properly and promptly.

*"A project is complete when it starts working for you,
rather than you working for it."*
– SCOTT ALLEN

1 Walker, Greg, "Definitions of Conflict: An Academic Sampler," *Conflict Management in Higher Education Report*, 2005, < http://www.campus-adr.org/CMHER/ReportResources/Definitions.html> (December 17, 2007).

2 Panic-attacks.co.uk, "Part 5: The Brain and Panic Attacks: Emotional Hijacking," *The Panic Attack Prevention Program*, 2001-2006, <http://www.panic-attacks.co.uk/panic_attacks_5.htm /> (July 26, 2006).

3 Dave Gerber, *Use Conflict: Advance Your Winning Life*, Timeless Publishing, 2007, p. 30-31.

4 Dave Gerber, *Use Conflict: Advance Your Winning Life*, Timeless Publishing, 2007.

5 Ibid., (back cover).

6 Dave Gerber and Pamela Leech, *Life Without Conflict: Introduction to a Winning Life*, Timeless Publishing, Springfield, VA, 2006, p. 8-10.

7 *The Guide to the Project Management Body of Knowledge*, 3rd Edition, ©2004 Project Management Institute.

II.
Twenty Points for Success
in Project Management

"The real leader has no need to direct –
he is content to point the way."
– HENRY MILLER

There is no single quality, trait or tenet that, if present, will assure success. Life, work and managing projects just aren't that simple. However, there are a few things to remember that if applied, will benefit the project manager, the organization and the project. The following may never be found in a User's Guide or corporate handout or a project charter, but they are important to remember. Adherence to these 20 points is consistent with becoming and remaining a successful project manager. We present these 20 points here, early in the book, because they are at the very core of our role as leaders. From portfolio to program to project and team, it will always be our abilities to communicate, inspire and lead that will separate poor from good and good from great.

Always Act with Integrity and Honesty.

These 20 points are in no particular order except for this first one! This one is non-negotiable. One either has it or does not. One either demonstrates integrity and honesty or does not. As professionals who represent not only ourselves but also our company, clients and customers, we can settle for nothing less than integrity and honesty in **all** we do **at all times**. What we allow can quickly become our standard. Project Management Professionals also have a professional code of conduct and a responsibility to act ethically; even when no one is looking.

Respond.

Actually, we like the word "**respondability**." This is one trait that separates us from the pack. When we are totally responsive to our client's needs, and the needs of those around us, we become value-added and an indispensable partner. To be responsive means being available, being prepared to carry out a mission on short or no notice and doing so in a positive and professional manner. Clients may not always notice when we are responsive but they *absolutely* notice when we are not. Responsiveness and respondability also apply to our co-workers and teammates in need. Help one another whenever we can; the next one to need help may be one of us.

Anticipate.

We have to think like our sponsors, clients, supervisors, and teammates think and before they do, if possible. When we can anticipate their next question or next requirement or anticipate the next turn in the road that they may not have considered, we add value. Think over the horizon. What may happen next and what does anticipating that possibility do to enhance preparation and reaction? Anticipation is more than having an idea of what is coming next, is also taking ACTION. When we sense an unplanned milestone briefing or presentation developing, prepare a draft for the client. Don't give her a blank page, give her something to ponder, change and play with. She will appreciate the thinking ahead and saving her some work. It is far easier to edit than to create so we are providing a great service when we take the lead and get out in front of requirements.

Follow-up.

We have all heard of "an action passed is an action completed." That is not the way it works, especially in project management when time is critical. When we start an action, it is OURS until it is completed. An action that we touch should nag at us until we know it is completed.

Don't assume someone else took it over. Check on it, help move it along and stay on top of it. We are accountable for it—and only us. Another aspect of the Follow-Up tenet is to close the loop with the people around us. When we are asked a question, answer it. When someone is clearly expecting to hear from us, be sure they do. Remember how frustrating it is when we have asked our sponsor a question, sought guidance or wanted clarification before moving forward and the lack of response (and evidently interest) is deafening?! Don't be guilty of the same lack of follow-up with those in our world.

Identify Problems *and* Solutions.

As professionals, we are expected to develop and offer solutions to problems we encounter and identify. When we see a problem and pass it along to our sponsor, boss or client without offering a course of action or two to address it, our value is limited. Think about the root causes of the problem, what can be enacted now and in the future to overcome, mitigate or avoid the problem and suggest solutions. When we play a role in shortening the time between problem identification and solution, we become known as a problem solvers, and we become more valuable to the organization.

Demonstrate Personal Accountability.

When we receive an action item or are given a responsibility, our leaders will rightfully hold us ACCOUNTABLE for it. There will be times that we will have to depend on others for help or input or other support to complete the action but we must appreciate that regardless of all that, in the end, we are accountable. We can't walk away and point the finger at someone else who failed us; it was ours to do. So, we will need to muster all of our personal and professional skills and use them to get the support we need to be successful. This is often quite a challenge.

Work Hard.

This should go without saying but here it is anyway. The work we do is not always a pleasure cruise; sometimes it's fun and energizing but sometimes it is just hard work. Be grateful when we work in an environment that notices hard work and recognizes when that extra effort is applied. We can't shy away from hard work. We are compensated for the work we do so always give it 100% effort and we will never be faulted. Remember the wise words of the baseball manager in A League of Their Own, "...if it was easy, everyone would do it."

Show a Sense of Urgency.

We have to maintain a healthy sense of urgency about our work. This not only keeps the interest high and the adrenaline flowing, it demonstrates our level of concern for the project and mission at hand. Nothing is more painful to watch than project manager or project team member half-stepping his or her way through the day. Most anyone can spot it in a minute and those who are pumping along tend to resent those who take on work like it was the Ebola virus. We must get our work done as quickly as we can and show everyone that we care about the task. That pep in our step is another discriminator that separates us from everyone else.

Foster Personal Discipline.

Be professional. Be on time, be prompt for meetings, dress properly, be prepared wherever we go and don't do anything to embarrass ourselves, our project teammates or the company we represent. More and more emphasis is placed on this trait these days, maybe because it seems to be in shorter supply than in the past. Strive to be the kind of person that others will look up to. We should set the bar high for ourselves and we will never regret the reaction we get from others or the improved results we derive from within.

Lead by Example and Follow Well and Faithfully.

One does not have to hold a formal leadership position to be a leader. In fact, leaders and leadership are distinctive. Certainly good leaders exhibit sound leadership traits and adhere to its key principles, yet these leadership traits can be found in just about anyone. The best leaders lead by example. We should be ever vigilant in looking for these burgeoning leaders around us and on our teams. Identifying and nurturing the next generation of leader is one of the most important responsibilities of any leader. Leadership also brings some baggage. Everyone watches everyone so we must be sure what we are demonstrating is what we really want to portray—a capable, confident professional who does his or her job to the best of his or her ability—all day, every day.

The military has long had an axiom that one is "on parade 24 hours a day." Remember that and act accordingly. Take charge when necessary and do so with confidence. Don't be surprised when others follow. They will. Learn how to be a good follower too.

Everyone has a boss, and our roles as followers can make or break our leaders and affect the overall success of the entire project. Good followers grow into good leaders because they understand the other side of the equation. Followership is more than taking orders and doing what we are told. It's adhering to norms, being part of the team and encouraging others to join in the undertaking to achieve a common goal. A project without good followers is a doomed effort.

Be Loyal in All Directions.

This means being loyal to our employer, our supervisor, our co-workers and our subordinates. This is one of those traits that will always cut both ways. It is pretty basic but is often absent or situationally dependent. Loyalty means we don't partake in rumor mongering and we don't trash others behind their back. Professional disagreements are one thing but backstabbing and the like is disloyalty and it cheapens those who engage in it. Loyalty does not imply that one should be "blinded" by it; not at all. Do what's right while being loyal to those around us. If we feel we must go in another direction, we need to be open and candid with our reasons and then do so, but we have to guard against being underhanded or perceived to be slick.

Be Consistent.

Leaders and project managers are becoming more and more unpredictable. This may be a function of volatile environments, constant changes in scope and timelines and staffing movements, but the results can be devastating to team morale and performance. Sometimes misdiagnosed by team members or subordinates as mere mood swings, the inconsistent behavior of the leader is disheartening and debilitating and increases the instances of fear—in this case, fear of unknown consequences. Solid leaders are consistent and unambiguous. Though some variance in response and reaction is understandable, it should be uncommon.

Show Gratitude and Respect for Others.

The Golden Rule applies and they don't call it golden for nothing. "Do unto others, as you would have them do unto you." Respect one another as individuals and we will be respected in return – it's that simple. Some have coined the PLATINUM RULE, "Do unto others as they would like to be done unto." This requires some real people skills and the desire to extend oneself. Respect is one of those unusual commodities that one can only receive by giving.

Build Teamwork and Collaboration.

Imagine…Teamwork as a critical element in successful projects? Remember, we are not alone. We should never spend time banging our head on the wall because we feel isolated and alone in our work and can't get ahead of it. Find a teammate, co-worker, supervisor—anyone—and ask for help. Usually, the response will be very positive, even surprising. It's tempting to feel vulnerable and insufficient if we need to ask for help, but we can't allow that to stop us. In the circle of life, we will find ourselves on the opposite side of this equation at some point. Get things done together, may be just one-on-one. Learn to work together towards a solution. Give and take. Very few people can accomplish great things alone—in fact, it's doubtful anyone ever has. It does take cooperation and collaboration to succeed, so we must extend our reach and permit others to reach out to us to foster true success. Great project teams are the result of rigorous collaboration!

Promote a Common Purpose.

We can call this our vision. Good leaders recognize that with no visible, achievable or defined target, even well-intended actions are essentially random and arbitrary. Leaders help identify the common purpose and unify the team members to move toward that target. They provide the goal and the means to get there. It can be challenging, but a key role of leadership is explaining how all the disparate parts need to work in concert to achieve success. Without the common purpose defined, teams could find themselves working at less than peak efficiency or worse—working against one another.

Infuse Passion.

We have all heard much said about the benefits of having a passion for our life's work. It is true. We need to get passionate about what we are doing. We must learn to appreciate that what we do makes a difference in the lives of real people out there. If we can't feel energetic and enthused and upbeat about spending our day trying to make things better (systems, relationships, and so on), then we need to check for a pulse. This is great and noble work and we should be proud of our daily contributions to the cause.

Cultivate Our Reputation.

We are our reputation. We should be asking, "What does ours say about us?" Work every day to improve it by doing what is right and taking care of one another. We must over-extend ourselves to our clients, our customers and our co-workers. When we do this, our reputation will speak volumes. We must keep this in mind…its not *who's* right, it's *what* is right that is important.

Display a Seriousness of Purpose and a Sense of Humor.

Take the job seriously. Work hard at becoming better at it. Study what we need to learn to become proficient and competent. Work is a serious business and others will be depending on us knowing our job. Project management is ever-evolving and changing to meet the emerging demands of a growing economy and diverse workforce. Keep reading, learning and applying what is learned. Work is serious but we still need to have fun! Let's keep our sense of humor at all costs! Use it to diffuse tense situations but be careful to use it appropriately—never to hurt someone else. No matter how hard the day or how long the hours, it could always be worse. We rarely have bleeding and death to contend with so keep things in perspective.

Continue to Grow.

We are responsible for our development and growth as a person and professionally. Others may be around to help with training, education and job placement when appropriate, but we each need to take responsibility for discovering what we want to be and how we want to get there. When we stop growing, we die.

Care for Those in Your Charge.

As a leader or project manager, nothing is more defining than the way we take care of those in our service. We must set and maintain high standards for ourselves and our people. Enforce those standards of behavior and performance. When we obviously care for those on whom we depend, we will, in turn, be cared for by them.

These "20 Points" have appeared in various forms, publications and presentations over the years. They are universal in nature and applicable across nearly any work endeavor. As we wrote "Are You the King or Queen of Conflict in Project Management," it quickly became evident that they have tremendous resonance in the world of managing and leading projects and programs. They have been further adapted here for this purpose.

"A good manager doesn't try to eliminate conflict;
he tries to keep it from wasting the energies of his people.
If you're the boss and your people fight you openly
when they think you are wrong – that's healthy."
– ROBERT TOWNSEND

III.
F.A.C.T.S.™

"Wisdom consists of the anticipation of consequences."
– NORMAN COUSINS

FEAR * ANGER * CONTROL * TRUST * SYNERGY

We believe that fear, anger, control, lack of trust and synergy are the greatest inhibitors to a project manager's life and ability to successfully carry out his or her leadership duties.[8] Before explaining each concept in its own individual chapter we wanted to begin with questions for consideration.

We will use the Agents of Socialization, the Essential Questions and our past experiences to explore each of these concepts and how they directly relate to us. Then we will dive into each chapter to further understand how each variable and emotion directly impacts our work.

F = Fear

- When leading projects and obstacles between us and other professionals' begin to surface; is our first response fight or flight? Why?
- What is our approach toward handling disputes or dealing with conflict?
- What fears get in the way of successfully leading projects at a very high competency level, all the time?

A = Anger

- How does anger get in the way?
- How does our anger show up as a "button" that people can push?
- Who taught us to be angry?
- Who taught us what to do with our anger?

C = Control

- What elements of controlling projects do we do well? Poorly?
- How do we feel when someone tries to control something within our territory and how do we respond?
- How do our "control buttons" get pushed and when does it happen the most?

T = Trust

- Who can we trust all the time?
- What is a working definition of trust that feels right for us?
- How do we define, establish and maintain trust over time?

S = Synergy

- How well do we lead others to create synergy?
- How well do we work with others when we are not the final decision maker?
- In what ways can synergy be created if relationships start to spiral downward?

Overview of our PMBOK Guide Infrastructure

In crafting this book, we considered several approaches. Our challenge to meld the key components of conflict with the essential elements of project management was critical. We have created such a "matrix" with one axis representing the conflict aspects of F.A.C.T.S. (Fear, Anger, Control, lack of Trust and Synergy) and the other depicting the Nine Knowledge Areas prescribed by the PMBOK Guide (Project Integration, Scope, Time, Cost, Quality, Human Resources, Communications, Risk and Procurement Management).[9]

This cross-referencing permits a ready appreciation for the boundless sources of conflict for project managers. We can quickly see that conflict plays a fundamental role in managing projects and leading teams. Its mastery is an important step in achieving success in any endeavor involving more than a single person working independently.

"Surely, whoever speaks to me in the right voice,
him or her I shall follow."
— WALT WHITMAN

8 Dave Gerber, *Use Conflict: Advance Your Winning Life*, Timeless Publishing, 2007

9 *The Guide to the Project Management Body of Knowledge*, 3rd Edition,
   ©2004 Project Management Institute.

IV.
<u>Fear</u> and the Knowledge Areas

"Ultimately, we know deeply the other side of every fear is a freedom."
— MARILYN FERGUSON

What is fear?

Most dictionaries define fear in relation to feelings of apprehension, calamity, and dread. Experientially, fear has to do with the feeling that something unpleasant or even terrible is going to happen. A moment's reflection shows, however, that fear involves far more than our feelings. It also involves our mind and body. A moment's reflection also shows us that there are many levels of fear.[10]

We live in a fear-based society. Think about the products we are sold— tires to protect the babies that ride in our cars, deodorant to keep us from being offensive, make-up to hide our imperfections. The list goes on and on. Consider how many media advertisements in our society try to get us to be afraid of something in order for us to see greater value in their product. Unfortunately in the U.S., that mentality has permeated our collective unconscious. We walk around with a generalized sense of fear.[11] As project mangers, this can be the most deadly form of self-destructive, passive behavior. The fear of failure is pervasive at the workplace and may even be heightened in a project setting. Consider the stakes and the circumstances. Projects are inherently short-lived (relatively speaking), with constrained budgets, schedules and limited human resources.

Just about every aspect of the work of the conscientious project manager will, in some way, be governed, or at least influenced by fear. It follows then, that this fear should be addressed by the project manager openly and candidly at some point in the process. Though this may not be the time for open confession of the existence of fear, it will be useful for the manager to acknowledge it to him/herself. Recognizing the existence of the "fear factor" is in itself, helpful. It permits the leader to move forward while addressing the fear of failure during the process.

Other fears exist in greater and lesser degrees for the project manager and team members as well. The fear of success – yes the *fear of success* is real. "If I can complete this project on time and save money and exceed expectations, I may be given more or tougher projects in the future." Not everyone wants that "reward." It's important to understand that very real fear in those on whom we depend. Others include the fear of disenfranchisement or estrangement from the group, the fear of ridicule, the fear of being found out (that we are in well over our head) and the fear of having to absorb the wrath of a colleague or supervisor. So, facing these fears and working through them becomes critical to our collective and individual success. Imagine how difficult it may be for the project manager to strive deliberately for success while at the same time fearing its achievement. The conflict that emerges from operating out of fear can be debilitating, even destructive, so it must be understood and managed.

What kind of fears do people face in general? Which of these are common among professionals and project managers? After countless brainstorms and introspective sessions with many people, we believe the following represent people's common fears. As described in Dave Gerber's book, *Use Conflict: Advance Your Winning Life*, these are:

- *Rejection*
- *Public speaking*
- *Disapproval*
- Taking airplane trips
- *Not meeting expectations*
- Dogs
- Darkness
- Seeing someone bleed
- *Test taking*
- Dentists, doctors and hospitals
- *Making mistakes*
- *People displaying anger*
- Injections
- Spiders
- *Being late*
- Drowning
- Dying young
- Police
- Growing old alone

All of the ones listed in *italics* relate to the fear of being judged. We fear being judged because we do not want to have to explain ourselves or measure up to someone else's subjective, individual standards that in fact, may impose huge costs on our personal and professional lives.

In our informal conversations with project managers in several career fields, one constant theme emerged in discussions about fear...fear is really about the unknown. How will team members perform, will we meet budget requirements, and what unplanned obstacles will require the swift implementation of a yet undeveloped contingency plan? Because there are so many unknowns and variables that are beyond our control, fear often invades our rational thinking. In reality, however, it serves no useful purpose while causing unnecessary anxiety and distress.

When talking with project managers, it became clear that most generalized fear in the industry fell into specific categories. These include the fear of:
1. Failure to achieve the mission (in over our head, mismatched resources, aggressive schedule, etc.)
2. Experiencing a major problem of some kind without sufficient resources or experience to overcome it
3. Exposure to a safety risk to team members (physical, interpersonal, emotional etc...)
4. Overcoming poor relationship issues among team members or with the client/sponsor
5. Poor performance resulting in not getting future work

Project managers, perhaps more than most, work hard to eliminate the fear factor. The principal vehicle for this effort is the project plan. Nothing goes farther toward limiting the effects of fear than a well thought out, detailed plan with built in contingency operations, alternate approaches and revised timelines. The project management plan provides the road map for successful completion of the project – on that we can all agree. But, once the first meeting is held, the first paper is drafted, or the first deadline is missed, the plan that we counted on to anchor us in tough times and help us navigate to the end—*changes*.

Fear starts to creep in. Untended, it grows stronger and begins to affect our thinking, our reaction to more changes and soon enough, fear takes over. Fear becomes our single most significant motivation and our project is now in serious jeopardy. When we are motivated by fear, our reasoning changes and our intellect no longer serves us well. We start to think about completion and not about success.

Using the PMBOK Guide as described in the overview chapter, the following text examines how FEAR plays a role in each of the nine knowledge areas in the world of project management. As we recall our own experiences in this new context, we begin to see where several elements of fear can invade our thinking and affect our actions.

	Fear	Anger	Control	Trust	Synergy
Integration					
Scope					
Time					
Cost					
Quality					
Human Resources					
Communication					
Risk					
Procurement					

1. Integration

Fear, especially at the outset of a project or any endeavor, can be immobilizing. As we proceed through all stages of integration management, we will face the inevitable concerns of every leader – how will we manage change?

A fully functioning integration management plan ensures that the team is adhering to the approved project plan and its varied processes. Concern can deepen into fear fairly easily and quickly once the team appears to be even the slightest bit off track. Here, the manager must effectively deal with change management and change control and lead the team while demonstrating confidence in the plan and the established control mechanisms already developed.

2. Scope

Scope creep! We are not sure there has ever been a project that was free of scope creep. The fear of being ill-prepared for additional requirements can lead to poor operational and strategic decisions by the project manager. Some "creep" is acceptable, as long as its fully understood by all parties and most importantly, the project sponsor, that the process, players, cost and outcome are now subject to necessary refinement. Scope creep differs from controlled changes. We can effectively plan for controlled changes that affect nearly all plans. Creep can occur when we lose focus on the plan, stop paying keen attention to detail or allow others to make decisions or assumptions that belong to us.

3. Time

Most project managers fear there is never enough time, and with good reason—there rarely is! Counting on other people to meet their deadlines over which the project manager can exercise little control, is commonplace. Certainly, contingency plans have been crafted and can be initiated, schedules can be uniformly altered and updated, but this typically adds costs and can impact quality. The risks are high and the reward is questionable—will there EVER be sufficient time? Honest mistakes made by competent people combine with dozens, if not hundreds of other variables and force us to constantly be mindful of the one commodity that cannot be replaced; time.

4. Cost

The fear of delivering poor initial estimates resulting in cost overruns is part of the life of the project manager. It is clearly difficult to completely identify every key aspect of the requirement presented by a given project deliverable schedule. We estimate using a number of formulas, past experience and known variables. Yet, we will be wrong in our estimate, hence our planned budget will need to change. Further, it's a safe bet we won't have misjudged in our favor, so the negative impact of our error and the resulting increase in costs to our sponsor can cause the fear of failure to escalate quickly.

5. Quality

Being responsible for the overall "health" of the project is most challenging. The project manager must develop and install a viable quality control plan with appropriate and sufficient metrics to monitor the project to ensure its deliverables meet the standards set forth in the charter. While managing change, scope creep and costs, quality can become vulnerable to oversight. Project managers lose sleep over quality concerns during integration because of the risk of missing a key quality standard while trying to maintain all the other requirements.

6. Human Resources

Here the reevaluation of the proper allocation of scarce, and probably expensive human resources, can cause alarm for any project leader. Beyond the numbers and the distribution of work, is the requirement to team build and resolve conflicts among team members without impacting the success of the project. We also worry that we have the right mix of talent, experience and capabilities to staff a winning team. Over time, this concern may fade, but as new project members come aboard and other key members depart, the issues of team chemistry ebb and flow and must be continually managed.

7. Communication

Show us a project manager who is a poor communicator and we will show a failing project manager and a project at significant risk. Unfortunately, this is not an unusual occurrence. Communication skills, particularly interpersonal communication skills, are at a premium in today's project workforce. Communicating the plan is critical, but less difficult—even for a relatively poor communicator.

Show the plan, identify the communication links and milestones and we are on the way. The real effort and the fear come in to play when the project manager must admonish or counsel a team member and is not prepared to do so. It may be tempting to put this discussion off indefinitely, for fear of upsetting the team member or facing a direct challenge, but project managers must learn to face this key element of leadership and to do so with confidence.

8. Risk

Perhaps nothing equates more quickly to fear than risk. All projects suffer from risk at one point or another. The project manager's risk mitigation planning is crucial to effectively handling the results of risks as they arise. A solid plan that addresses potential risk factors and the intended methods to overcome them will reduce the anxiety of the team, the sponsor and the leader. This allows the group to focus on following the plan, with the knowledge that if and when risk factors arise, they will be dealt with as planned.

9. Procurement

In many instances, procurement of additional products or services will be necessary to complete the project. To mitigate the effects of fear of failure here, the effective project manager should develop and maintain professional working relationships with those vendors important to the project. There will be less to fear, knowing that a workable procurement plan is in place, the key players know one another and work well together and schedules are fully integrated. Not paying attention to the nuances of procurement management, the responsible parties involved and the procurement rules for one's industry or government sector can be costly. Knowledge mitigates fear.

"Collective fear stimulates herd instinct,
and tends to produce ferocity toward those who
are not regarded as members of the herd."
— BERTRAND RUSSELL

10 Dennis Lewis, "Transforming Fear," *Natural Breathing for Health, Well-Being, Longevity and Self-Revitalization*, December 27, 2007. <http://www.authentic-breathing.com/transforming_fear.htm> (December 29, 2007).

11 Dave Gerber, p. 48; *Use Conflict: Advance Your Winning Life*, Timeless Publishing, 2007.

V.
Anger and the Knowledge Areas

"He [or she] who angers you conquers you."
— ELIZABETH KENNY

Anger, however it is defined, it truly is an emotion we can almost do without. Anger is "an emotional state that varies in intensity from mild irritation to intense fury and rage," says Charles Spielberger, PhD. in a brochure published by the American Psychological Association.[12] Anger gets in the way, blinds us to other's realities, clouds judgment and usually, fundamentally, works against our own needs and interests.

With anger there are often physiological changes. If we get angry, our heart rate increases and blood pressure, adrenaline levels, and energy hormones all start to rise. Anger comes from deep inside and can take many forms, especially if it has been suppressed over time. How often, as a project manager, does our present anger stem from a chain of events that happened in the past? Our experience in dealing with anger can often govern how we will deal with it now and in the future.

Project managers, like many in leadership positions, will often choose to avoid conflict early in relationships or early in the course of a project or task. This approach, though non-threatening at the time, only sets the stage for the inevitable conflict that will likely be more volatile having grown unattended over time.

In life, as in projects, things go wrong. It's easy to blame our anger on other people...and we often do. Though we control our own emotions; even if other people "push our buttons" or emotions get triggered...we can easily become emotionally hijacked, as described in Essential Question #1.

Before, during or after a project task, we can get hijacked; losing our ability to be creative, think logically and sequentially, control our breathing, reason effectively and more. Before the task, we are concerned that we have a clear understanding of the requirement and if we will have sufficient resources to meet that need. During the execution of the task, those worries continue and may mount. We add the concerns of time management, schedule integration and scope creep and more problems emerge. Once completed, we fret over details not addressed, inconclusive results, incomplete task elements, team frustrations and the fear of failure and starting over.

Anger can be such a powerful force in our lives that we tend to take it out on ourselves, physically. When the body senses anger, violence or aggression, it provides itself a large shot of adrenaline. While this is normal, it often happens without us knowing it, feeling it, or preparing ourselves to deal with it. The impact of the adrenaline unload cannot be stopped by even most experienced conflict masters. So many people choose to suppress it instead. In doing so, they internalize the anger and will often project or transfer it to other people in the form of outward judgments, sarcasm, put downs and in extreme instances, maybe even violence.

When someone is using anger as a crutch or device of control on a project team, they may become negative, short-fused, judgmental, resentful, and uncooperative. They may use cynical humor, be unsympathetic toward others, or be irritable, unforgiving and argumentative.

We found that the main triggers for anger could be categorized:

Interpersonal Conflict

- Innate differences
- Communication styles
- Stepping out of the chain of command
- Incident of some kind that threatens the mission or relationships
- Misinterpreted or real threat to needs
- Misinterpreted or real threat to resources
- Having to step into a conflict between team members or
  team members and the client

Team Members Not Meeting Deadlines

- Deadlines and declarations not met
- Lack of accountability
- Top Cover for the "Rocks" (ineffective team members)
- Self-imposed obstacles by individuals or the team
- Public ridicule
- Failure to select the right people for the job
- Poor planning
- Poor presentation of ideas (particularly if done to the client)
- Team members not stepping up to help others and risking mission failure

Human Error

- Miscalculations
- Poor planning
- Safety issues
- Poor execution of good planning
- The negative results and explosion after the "Normalization of Deviance"[13]
- Cyclical Phenomenon
- "It worked before without problems"
- Rationalization
- Lack of individual thinking
- "Why wasn't this caught?" – mental error
- Group think

Managing our anger can reduce the associated emotional feelings and physiological stimulation most often detrimental to the situation or the relationships involved. A key to anger management is the core belief that we cannot change other people, their behaviors or statements. We can only control our responses to them.

There is a clear distinction between intention and behavior. We often feel anger when we have not taken the time to slow down and to think about the circumstance that is making us angry. Exactly why are we angry right now? Was the person that made us angry intending to do so? Was their behavior congruent with their intentions? Are we mistakenly getting angry for no reason, simply because we reacted too quickly to what we thought was happening?

When we slow down to investigate someone's behavior, and then try to understand the original intention, we find there is a difference. Usually we are pleasantly surprised to reflect that while the behavior looked "ugly" or made us angry, often people actually had positive intentions.

Another key is to know what to do with ourselves when anger arises— how to find calm. In this state we can better control our internal responses and transition to logic and the ability to accurately express ourselves. Eventually we will be able to prevent the destructive feelings anger creates within us.

Again, the PMBOK Guide's nine knowledge areas cross-referenced with our understanding of ANGER opens up many doors and encourages exploration of some previously unexamined issues. Once we acknowledge our experiences with the feelings of anger that may accompany our work as project managers, it becomes apparent that our need for improved anger management skills is vital to our survival and our success.

	Fear	Anger	Control	Trust	Synergy
Integration					
Scope					
Time					
Cost					
Quality					
Human Resources					
Communication					
Risk					
Procurement					

1. Integration

Sometimes a lack of cooperation can plague a project manager and the project itself. It can be immensely frustrating for the leader to feel like he or she is fighting an uphill battle all the way because some team members just "don't get it." One can start to feel as if they have been set up for failure and are essentially acting alone. Anger can be aroused, and left untended, will separate the leader from the offending teammate or the entire team in some cases. Dealing with changes throughout the life of the project will test the temperament of even the most stoic project manager. Being aware of this potential source of frustration can help to address it effectively.

2. Scope

"This isn't in the original Scope Statement! How can I be expected to produce this now, with limited resources, less time and…?" This may sound familiar to anyone who has led a project of just about any consequence. It's easy to become angry when we are being asked (or directed) to do more with less. Effectively managing scope is difficult, but again, planning for this eventuality goes a long way to preventing meltdown when the requirements escalate.

3. Time

The natural shortage of time (a project management variation on Murphy's Law that everything takes longer than planned) is a sure cause for rising resentment and anger on the part of the project leader. We may feel as if we just can't give the project our best effort if we don't have the time to do it right. We sense that our reputation may be at risk because of this and we get exasperated. We must be careful that this anger does not show in front of the project team, lest it begin to permeate the entire group and only add to our challenges. Planning for time constraints allows us to more effectively work through them when we have no other alternative.

4. Cost

We have found through our research that some project sponsors have difficulty differentiating between cost and value. What we may think is a reasonable expense to see the project through, the owner may consider "gold plating" and unnecessary.

In other cases, our costs of doing business may be out of our immediate control (more on that later). Anger sets in when we feel blamed for increased costs when it wasn't our doing. For example, material costs for a construction project may rise during certain seasons and because we may be over on our timeline, we are facing cost hikes for which we had not planned. Not our fault, but it comes back on us as managers and we have to set that irritation aside to effectively lead the team. Successful project leaders are effective at managing the expectations of the client, sponsor and stakeholders.

5. Quality

There are times in the life of a project when, notwithstanding solid quality assurance planning and effective quality control measures, we miss the mark. Our first reaction is often anger. We are upset with ourselves, our team members and the circumstances that caused the quality failure. We are frustrated for not thinking of everything and risking our collective reputation on, of all things, a poor product or shoddy service. We grow more angry realizing that we are now at a greater risk of losing business—no one wants to hire a project manager that may get the work completed on schedule but delivers a substandard product. It's important to control that anger, redirect it toward crisis management and improvement measures we can share with the project sponsor. Often, a professional response to these kinds of challenges brings about a positive result we would never have foreseen or planned.

6. Human Resources

If circumstances can generate anger, just think about how easily we can be angered by the people around us. As the project leader, we may feel that some of our key stakeholders or teammates are disengaged and placing the project (and us) at risk. We may come to believe that we don't have the right team in place or that we may not be the best leader for the project. We can be easily provoked when we sense that the very people on whom we must depend, are not on the same page as we are.

7. Communication

Frustrations over miscommunication are prevalent in the workplace and certainly within and across projects. With the emergence of new communication media, such as e-mail, text messaging, "blogging" and shared Websites, the challenges of communicating clearly and effectively are greater and greater. When what we said is not what was heard – we can and often do get angry. We can mitigate this by more face-to-face meetings but these are not always practical. It really requires all members of the team, particularly the leader, to take measures to ensure the message is clear and is understood.

Deborah Tannen discusses an important concept around communication that deals with messages and meta-messages. People can either have a problem with the message or the method by which the communiqué was sent. If one were to imagine the unintended and undesired consequences of providing repeated validation to a valued project manager…but *only* doing it by e-mail.

She continues to argue that people actually code their message in their own version of the language, only to be decoded by someone using their personal version of the same language. In short, we have all experienced what it feels like to misinterpret a message or see the reaction from others who did not understand the intended meaning. What this means is that language is fragile; it can be misinterpreted easily; this mistake, honest or not, can cause anger, resentment, trust issues and more.[14]

8. Risk

Many of us have gone from disappointment to anger when project sponsors don't appreciate the effects of insisting on operating in a "zero risk" environment. Risk is a fact of any project and comes in many forms, from funding to political decisions to the weather.

As project leaders, we need to make the customer or sponsor feel comfortable with risk and our ability to address problems as they arise. Again, communication is important and will help to ease tensions that can be manifested by angry outbursts.

9. Procurement

Ill-defined requirements are an endless source of frustration for project managers. Poorly written statements of work, unclear task statements and confusing or even contradictory language adds time to the process and can result in a poor outcome. We need to do all we can as project managers to help the sponsor identify the desired end-state, consider the tools necessary to deliver that product or service and provide the environment that sets the tone for success.

As project managers procuring services for our team, we must be equally vigilant about clarity in the requirements development stage. We have to be careful what we ask for – we may get it. We must return to the importance of effective communication to reduce the opportunity for poor procurement activities and the resulting anger and frustration that causes.

"We boil at different degrees."
— RALPH WALDO EMERSON

12 John McManamy, "Anger and Depression in Bipolar Disorder," *McMan's Depression and Bipolar Web*, n.d., <http://www.mcmanweb.com/anger.htm> (July 26, 2006).

13 Mike Mullane, "The Challenger Launch Decision," 1996 <http://www.mikemullane.com> (December 31, 2007).

> **Normalization of Deviance** is the result of allowing incremental changes to previously hard and fast requirements to become the new standard. The fact that these changes may seem rather inconsequential at the time makes them easier to overlook or accept, though the result of each of these changes or all of them combined can lead to drastically different results than originally expected or required. Continually redefining what is acceptable based upon what negative behaviors have not happened...fundamentally doesn't make sense and it could, in some cases, even cost lives.

14 Deborah Tannen, "Survival Guide: Deborah Tannen, linguist and professor", *Personal Interview*, Washington Technology, 1105 Government Information Group, 11/04/02; Vol. 17 No. 16, http://www.washingtontechnology.com/print/17_16/19426-1.html

VI.
<u>Control</u> and the Knowledge Areas

*"You are searching for the magic key that will unlock the door
to the source of power; and yet you have the key in your own hands,
and you may use it the moment you learn to control your thoughts."*
     – NAPOLEON HILL

What is control?

Control is when someone else attempts to exercise power, influence or authority over us, whether it is to faintly adjust, judge, regulate, argue, check, provide unsolicited feedback or even try to restrain us from doing something we have chosen, good or bad, right or wrong.

Project managers feel the "tug" of control from all types of constituents. It can often be a matter of priority, power, unknown circumstances, someone trying to manage the outcome, take command of the operation, and a whole lot more. As project managers, by definition, we are in control of our projects. However, there are several triggers that can lead us to react or respond in several different ways, impacting our ability to properly exercise that control. The themes that seem to most often set off the "control" response for project managers are:
- If we are willing to allow ourselves to feel controlled by others
- When someone tries to take over without permission
- When a member "jumps" the command chain
- When things go wrong, we feel out of control. These events include:
    - Emergencies
    - Required change orders
    - Changes based on emerging circumstances
    - When people do not behave as we anticipated
    - When people behave irrationally
    - When we allow others to push our control button
      (whether trying or not)

- Unreasonable statements of work or project charters
- Unclear statements of work or project charters
- Client or others wanting us to conduct the project differently than we desire
- When we feel like someone is an unnecessary obstacle to progress or project completion
- When someone gets in the way of our needs

There are countless things that are out of our control, and this list represents only a few recurring themes and "buttons" that get pushed (what seems like automatically) when we lead projects. Sometimes, frankly, it is not up to us alone.

While we are in control, we have others that are impacting how successful we will be. The leader's inability to meet timelines, budgets, or overcome interpersonal issues, among other failures, will ultimately lead to the project manager's demise. This is truly where the strength of our relationships with others comes in to play. How can we get other people to do what we want them to do, within the time we want it done, using the resources we have allocated for them - and like it? Much of this has to do with appearing to relinquish control by empowering team leads and employees. When we allow others to influence the project, its plan and its process and thus buy-in to the objectives of the project, their views and feelings are validated. When team members receive this recognition, they are more likely to actively participate and add value.

The PMBOK Guide's nine knowledge areas cross-referenced with our understanding of CONTROL can help to provide clarity on how this issue impacts us all, at very deep levels. Control issues are nothing new to project managers, yet we tend to internalize them and often allow them to "beat us up." Though we recognize our limitations relative to control, we often fail to effectively work through control challenges because we are not looking at them in the context of work, but rather in a more personal way.

	Fear	Anger	Control	Trust	Synergy
Integration					
Scope					
Time					
Cost					
Quality					
Human Resources					
Communication					
Risk					
Procurement					

1. Integration

As project managers fighting to consider all the salient points of project integration, adherence to the project plan and forward progress, we may find ourselves lacking the control we thought we had been awarded at the outset. Competing requirements, sponsor micro-management and perhaps even a lack of experience on our part can contribute to control issues here.

2. Scope

We have addressed the phenomenon of scope creep earlier and find that this unfortunate aspect of most projects permeates nearly all facets of project management. We may have accounted for all of the specified tasks for the project, but the client or sponsor almost always expects us to address the *implied* tasks as well. Scope statements are often incomplete and without continuous amendment, can quickly become fairly useless. We must meet the expectations of the sponsor, and if those include tasks that we never spelled out, so be it. All the forethought in the world won't eliminate the possibility that we are expected to do something that was not clearly articulated in the plan. We feel out of control and put upon, yet have few alternatives but to perform as expected.

3. Time

If the project manager has done a good job of defining activities, tasks, and sequencing and has considered legitimate duration estimates in his or her plan, control issues will be mitigated from the start. Promising too much too soon is the downfall of many a project manager. Better to promise a later delivery, come through earlier than expected and be a hero! We are not suggesting that we purposely mislead our sponsors at all – rather that we must consider all the factors that can and will impact our time estimates and provide a more realistic schedule for our project deliverables.

4. Cost

One of our primary responsibilities as a project manager is to control costs...this is relatively straight forward, yet inherently difficult. That said, what is often more difficult is commending other stakeholders to control their own costs. A project manager's ability to do this really isn't about numbers; it is about relationships and empowering individuals to be successful...most will do the "right thing."

In terms of controlling the financial resources assigned to the project, the project manager, with the support of the project sponsor, will typically plan for contingencies and set aside funds that may be required down the road. What? This doesn't happen? Well, not in the real world. We know that funds are scarce to begin with and without direct proof of a need, they won't be anywhere near our cost plan. It's up to the manager to plan for this, convince the sponsor of possible contingency requirements and then try to avoid that expense if possible.

5. Quality

Trying to control variables that impact project outcomes to produce high quality relationships, products and services is fundamental and the essence of our work as project leaders.

Each person on every team must first attain and sustain a 100% quality standard of themselves. Then, the project manager must employ his or her leadership abilities and communication skills to focus the team on the importance of maintaining quality standards.

Control and quality can be related to the way we work with people. If we want the benefits of high quality relationships, we may want to appear less controlling. This tactic requires us to strive to meet the needs of others early and often as a means to find win-win solutions.

6. Human Resources

Managing the human element on a project can be like herding cats at times. All the players have a mind of their own and a sense of their role on the team, the mission of the project and the contributions they can make to it. As the project manager, controlling all of these factors and melding the individuals into a team is one of the most difficult tasks of any leader. We certainly need to address their perspectives and perceptions of the project, seek their counsel and benefit from their expertise—after all, that's why they are on the team. The challenge is in keeping them focused, fulfilled, contributing and happy.

There are several techniques that can be used to better control the players. First and foremost it's essential to try to know and understand each team member and what value he or she brings to the effort. Next, we must communicate with each one in the way that works best for *them*, not necessarily us. Some people respond better to written direction while others prefer conversation. Some want one-on-one meetings and others prefer to meet as a team.

The variations are endless and not always logical or intuitive. The end result of controlling the human resources on our projects is to allow sufficient room for self-expression while ensuring that one's leadership position remains clearly understood and respected. This is a function that continues unabated throughout the project and can never be taken for granted.

7. Communication

How we control the way people speak and the flow of information makes a huge difference in the success of our day to day operations, short and long-term relationships as well as the final product.

It has been said that the individual who holds all the information and power, controls the solution. This is true and it is noteworthy to consider how much information we are willing to provide to others. If we appear to withhold information, offer shoddy explanations, lack confidence in our message or are simply dishonest...we are likely to generate far less input for the solution to meet the project manager's and the team's needs.

As project managers, we also need to consider how much information we can share and are willing to share. How does the dissemination of data, information and analyses influence all of the players; empower some; disenfranchise others, and help achieve the mission...without creating more conflict.

If people are given permission to share their ideas without judgment, be heard and feel respected with positive non-verbal communication, most will perform better, even if their ideas are not always actualized.

8. Risk

The Risk Management Plan, with all its faults, shortcomings and assumptions, is the best way to fend off the unknown in all projects. Experience in similar projects helps round out a better risk analysis, but we really do depend on some level of instinct to predict risk and develop work-arounds. Though it appears that the assumption of risk necessarily leads to less control, this is not at all the case. The identification of risk factors before and during the project life cycle serves to enhance our control.

9. Procurement

As a provider of project management support, we can become frustrated by the lack of control we can exercise over the procurement process that delivered the work to us. We were likely unable to influence the statement of work and as described earlier, can consequently suffer through poorly defined requirements while trying to describe how we will do the work.

The client too, can have issues with controlling the procurement process. Sometimes the sponsor or customer is forced by circumstances to go with the lowest cost, technically acceptable bid while this can clearly put the project at risk. Their frustration as owners over this lack of control rises when they have to face quality issues because funding was the key factor at the outset.

*"The shepherd always tries to persuade the sheep
that their interests and his own are the same."*
— STENDAHL

VII.
<u>Trust</u> and the Knowledge Areas

"Few delights can equal the mere presence
of one whom we trust utterly."
— GEORGE MACDONALD

Trust is the "assured reliance on the character, ability, strength, or truth of someone or something; one in which confidence is placed."[15]

Trust is a critical piece of currency for anyone managing projects or working on the team. Certainly, we must be able to rely on people to do their jobs and do them well. Competence is necessary. We need team members to meet their deadlines, actualize their declarations, work for more than themselves and support each other when things are difficult. The expectation of this enlightened viewpoint among the team members need not be out of line. Stated up front in the early stages of the initiating and planning phases, and revisited often during the course of the project, this level of mutual trust can absolutely be achieved and maintained.

The project manager can and should coordinate efforts; however it is up to each individual to build, maintain and sustain trust and trusting relationships. Without trust, people are less efficient, point fingers, dodge responsibility, give less than their best effort, "shop" the job market, create excuses and, simply, under-perform.

Some of the major themes that surfaced during conversations with project managers about what gets in the way of trust between them and the team include:
- Missed deadlines
- Excuses
- Hidden agendas
- Flat out lies and sight truths
- "Insider allies" – they bring unsolicited information for their own reasons

It is the responsibility of the project manager to not only trust team members, but to also create a trusting atmosphere where individuals in the group are more likely to take risks with trusted colleagues…this is vital!

The PMBOK Guide's nine knowledge areas cross-referenced with our understanding of the importance of TRUST will help us to better understand this form of "currency." As project managers, we must build, maintain and sustain trusting relationships that cover the entire web of stakeholders.

	Fear	Anger	Control	Trust	Synergy
Integration					
Scope					
Time					
Cost					
Quality					
Human Resources					
Communication					
Risk					
Procurement					

1. Integration
The stage for a successful project is set early on and reinforced throughout the life of the project. A principal component in this process is the thorough integration of all aspects of the work to be accomplished. It may be the ultimate responsibility of the project leader to ensure this is completed, but it will take all stakeholders involved to contribute to the effort to assure its success. Mutual trust and confidence among the team members will enhance and expedite this process.

The trusting relationships established from the beginning and honed throughout will be the bedrock for navigating through the trials and challenges brought by unexpected changes in direction, scope and funding, to name a few.

All stakeholders, led by the project manager, must think in the aggregate, unhitch from their own areas of special interest and support the larger mission. When an environment of mutual trust exists, this becomes the way normal project business is conducted.

2. Scope

Scope management, or mismanagement, has been the Achilles Heel for many a project manager. How can something we know to be naturally volatile and wrought with opportunity for disaster, still surprise us when we find ourselves overextended and under funded and under staffed? It may be that trained and tested project managers feel overconfident in their abilities to deal with unclear scope issues. It also may be that scope problems are often masked as other issues such as people problems and communication miscues. Trust plays another important role here as we struggle to manage and control project scope. We need to be sure from the outset, that we can not only trust the people who bring us information, but that we can trust the information itself.

Winning project managers ask a lot of questions and usually don't believe the first two or three answers are complete! If we are basing much of our planning and execution of the project on the legitimacy of the scope statement, it seems prudent to use all available means to validate the data and to be sure of the motives of the people sharing that data. Those trusting relationships we talked about earlier pay off now and can help assure smooth sailing in rough seas. But, we must keep in mind that even with the best of intentions, the people around us may deliver inaccurate information, culled from bad data that can drive us to faulty conclusions. Trust but verify—a great approach to most of what we do as project leaders.

3. Time

All we can trust about time is that it keeps moving. The ticking clock can be the worst nightmare for any project manager unless the project has been flawlessly planned and managed. Again, bad information about task duration will affect milestone management, cost, quality and a host of other factors critical to the success of the effort. Insist on hearing bad news in terms of time management. The only way it will come unabated is by first establishing an environment based on mutual trust.

4. Cost

Cost estimates carry an enormous amount of weight as we carry out each task and achieve each milestone. Solid estimates facilitate our control of events as they unfold before us and allow us to move from change to change with the knowledge that "we thought of this already and planned for this contingency." If we are able to trust our own experience as well as the experience of those feeding us information about cost, we will be more likely to succeed. Including all pertinent data, ensuring it is current and accurate, will help generate accurate estimates that in turn, earn us, as project managers, the trust of those around us.

5. Quality

Simply stated, high quality output builds trust while poor quality weakens it. Project sponsors, product users and project stakeholders of every kind rightly expect our commitment to quality. Our lack of attention to the caliber of our outcomes—focusing more on cost savings or completion time—will ultimately damage our reputation as project managers and ironically, increase our costs. Quality is at the forefront of the business world today, with both new and tested approaches, such as Six Sigma, the Balanced Scorecard and the Kaizen Model for continuous improvement, taking center stage as essential tools for leaders in every industry and throughout government. Trust is built on a foundation of quality and influences future purchases and association with the business. Producing a respectable product or service is (or should be) the driving force behind every discrete task and each adjustment to changing requirements. We have said that trust is hard to earn but easy to lose. Much of it depends on our ability to consistently and reliably deliver on our quality promises.

6. Human Resources

Many factors impact trust in any relationship. In projects, competence may be the single most important factor. Demonstration of competence as a project leader builds trust, instills loyalty and establishes the basis for all future working relationships. Our competence will be tested throughout any given project, to be sure. Our initial planning will or won't be validated, our estimates will prove to be accurate or off the mark, and our ability to effectively navigate through continuous change will be tested. This is why earning trust is so difficult and maintaining it is so tenuous. The team we create or inherit, as may be the case, will be our best resource for accomplishing the tasks and the ultimate mission. We have to show those who depend on us that we are competent and able and are deserving of their loyalty and trust. At the same time, we should be clear in our demonstration of our loyalty and trust outward to our team members and stakeholders. As in just about any relationship, mutual trust is the only trust that matters.

7. Communication

All project managers craft communication plans or refine existing plans for their purposes. Most of us recognize the importance of effective communication on the conduct and outcome of any group endeavor and take necessary steps to outline and practice how we will communicate with one another. We also establish when we will communicate and by what method and under what conditions. All are essential elements for staying on track, limiting miscues and avoiding missed opportunities. Yet, even the best communication plan is worthless if we cannot trust the content of the communication itself. Too often, leaders are told only the "green light" stories—nothing is yellow or red; all is well. Sometimes this is done out of fear and sometimes it's done just because it's easy and requires few questions. Successful project managers who have built a trusting and safe environment are far more likely to get the truth, even when the truth may be disappointing or even painful.

Another element related to trust and communication is the importance of sharing information. No good is served by keeping team members uninformed and in the dark. There are risks to this openness, of course, but the risks borne by hoarding information are far greater. Team members must be fully aware of the status of the project, upcoming events and milestones, key decision points, and our recommendations. All should be given the opportunity to form realistic expectations and to properly prepare themselves for inevitable changes. As leaders, we are privy to much information and it is our responsibility to share that information appropriately, responsibly and openly with those in our charge.

8. Risk

Risk and trust are two sides of the same coin. Trusting others naturally causes one to incur a certain amount of risk. We cannot escape the reality that we cannot do everything ourselves. We are facing increasingly complex problems and we are required to delegate responsibility to others to help us accomplish our missions. Clearly, we put ourselves, our reputations and the outcome of the project at some risk by doing so. Our trust in others, and theirs in us, is truly tested under these conditions. Do we delegate and disappear or do we pretend to delegate and then assume the position of chief overlord, watching and critiquing every move? These are hard choices but are made even more difficult when a suitable environment, based on trust, has not been established.

9. Procurement

If delegating and then trusting our teammates is difficult, trusting other service or product providers can be nearly impossible. Unless there is a long history of mutual trust and mutual gain between vendors, trust is not something to be expected too quickly. Sound procurement decisions and effective vendor management based on trust can separate the adequate project leader from the superior. We have to focus on the desired outcome and our key deliverables along the way. This focus will help us approach these important relationships in such a way as to foster trust and loyalty. These relationships, after all, will have a direct impact on the quality and timeliness of the product or service that we deliver to our customer.

"Trust only movement. Life happens at the level of events, not of words. Trust movement."
— ALFRED ADLER

15 <http://www.m-w.com/dictionary/trust> (October 17, 2007).

VIII.
Synergy and the Knowledge Areas

"None of us is as smart as all of us."
— KEN BLANCHARD

Synergy has a lot of definitions; we like to think of it as the combined energies of individuals that help to make up a group energy that helps everyone operate at a higher level. We have heard that 3x3 > 9 because as project managers we all know what it feels like when everything is "firing on all cylinders." Success seems to increase disproportionately or even exponentially when people are working together without conflict or are demonstrating the ability to use the conflict for a greater purpose. When ensuring people's dignity, showing respect for others and acting honorably… a group can achieve much more together than each individual can alone.

As a project manager, creating synergy is like leading an orchestra. Many of us have seen (and used) this metaphor in the past; that the orchestra leader does not play an instrument, but is essential to the success of the effort. Individually, the instruments may sound fine, but collectively and in harmony, they can produce a magnificent result.

The leader has a vision of what that end state should be, provides guidance to the players on how to get there as a group and helps them meld as a unified team—yet that orchestra leader still does not play a single note. It is his or her LEADERSHIP that provides the necessary environment for success. When any of the musicians is not on the same page (literally, in this case) as the rest of the unit, the disharmony is obvious and the sound is unpleasant.

Leading the orchestra and leading the project team is all about getting the best out of everyone, consistently…so results are achieved more quickly, at a level higher than expected by the audience or the client. This aspect of F.A.C.T.S. is truly about how to make individuals of all different kinds, click as a unit and meet or exceed the mission requirements.

When speaking with project managers on this subject, we identified a few prevailing themes about common obstacles to creating synergy and what helped to sustain it:

Obstacles to Synergy

- Lack of trust
- People's innate differences
- A team outsider
- Lack of follow through or accountability
- Emergency or crisis
- Outside distractions
- People's laziness – some don't want to pay the price for success

Helps to Create and Sustain Synergy

- Concerted effort to speak about it and behave in a way that creates it
- Individual's delivering upon expectations
- Team building and success rituals
- "Keeping it on the field"
- High level communication skills
- Consistency
- Understanding the importance of other's needs and interests
- Skilled and genuine active listening

As is implied, synergy doesn't "just happen." It is the bi-product of good leadership, followership, focus and working as a team to bring the diversity of minds together for the greater good...it is about reducing conflict, increasing efficiency, exceeding goals, learning from our worst and building upon our best practices.

Finally, there is the ever important connection between and among team members and stakeholders; we call it SYNERGY. The PMBOK Guide's nine knowledge areas woven with a better understanding of how high performance teams are built may help to clarify how this issue impacts us all...whether leading or following. Most of us can recall great and small professional triumphs, accomplished with others. These "wins" were achieved, in all likelihood, because the team was unified, focused and complimentary in their unique individual actions. More was accomplished as a fully functioning team than would have been possible alone.

	Fear	Anger	Control	Trust	Synergy
Integration					
Scope					
Time					
Cost					
Quality					
Human Resources					
Communication					
Risk					
Procurement					

1. Integration

What is integration, if not synergy in action? The very concepts of event, milestone and task integration, requires us to think in terms of alignment, harmony, unity and symbiosis. The project manager's greatest value can be found in his or her ability to properly fuse disparate elements of complex projects into a single, coherent and clear deliverable. When project integration is performed effectively at the outset of the project and revisited periodically during the other phases, the chances for success are increased exponentially. We have talked about the problems created by a stove-pipe approach to management. Information that fails to flow horizontally and diagonally may not get where it needs to go. By focusing on synergy and integration, we strengthen our chance for ultimate success.

2. Scope

We work very hard as project leaders to effectively manage scope. We spend a great deal of time in the early stages of our project definition to get the scope statement right. Why? Simply because we know both inherently and from hard experience, that insufficient scope management is like taking off on a trip with the wrong map. We will get somewhere eventually, but it won't be where we intended to go.

In fact, we may have made several unplanned side trips along the way because of poor scope management at the outset. In a synergistic approach, the project leader will call on his or her stakeholders, team members and sponsors to assist in the identification of scope issues and will lead the effort to define the project scope and articulate its limits.

Network diagrams, one of the many tools of the project manager, provide several types of resources to identify, plan and follow prescribed timelines. They also help us anticipate lag time and opportunities for increased efficiencies. Whether PERT or CPM or some other variation, these tools express the synergy that we strive for as projects progress through time. This synergy, to be real and useful, must be based on factual inputs, hard estimates and the realities of the project environment – not on hopes, dreams and fairy tales.

4. Cost

Project managers must ask (because their sponsors will ask) if the cost outlined for their project is appropriate for the stated mission. We may be tempted to understate the funding requirements for fear that our project will be vulnerable to elimination when money gets tight. On the other hand, we may tend to overstate the financial requirements for our project because we are concerned that we will get only a fraction of our requested amount – it runs the gamut.

Synergy, in terms of the cost element, must be achieved in several instances. First, the costs must align with the mission requirements and the timeline provided. Next, the team members and stakeholders and all parties involved need to be unified on the application of those costs across the project. Again, the health of the entire project must take precedence over any individual part. The manager will have to focus on harmonizing the individual tasks and deliverables into a synergistic and unified outcome – the outcome that was stated back when the project was initiated, unless otherwise altered.

5. Quality

It almost goes without saying that the ability to create and deliver a high quality project outcome, service or end product, relies on whether the team can generate and leverage the synergy created...early and often. When quality is perhaps the single most measurable deliverable, we cannot afford to allow it to go untended. Our quality assurance plans and quality control mechanisms will fail us if we have not first combined our collective energies toward defining what acceptable quality is and how it will be achieved. The realization of a quality outcome cannot be the result of a single notion by a single player – even the sponsor or project manager. Rather, the definition of a quality outcome must be the work of the collective, each bringing his or her own viewpoints, requirements and criteria to the table.

Working together is not enough. Working together in a way that brings out everyone's strengths *will* be enough. Pat Croce, former owner of the Philadelphia 76ers professional basketball team used to say that "results are a product of relationships." Further evidence that team development and team synergy in the world of sports reveals that this and other environments can provide valuable lessons. We all can learn a great deal about how winning teams function in any setting—sports, politics, the military, the business environment, and certainly within projects.

6. Human Resources

Let's be honest – we are far more likely to be happy and satisfied in our work and hence, more productive, when we are surrounded by people we like, or at a minimum, respect for their abilities to contribute to the common good. Here is where we see the truly high performing team exposed. Great teams, working in synergy, take it to a whole other level. The members of such teams know their own jobs and the jobs of the others on the team. They prepare incessantly, practice continually and execute flawlessly. Their work is seemingly effortless.

The leader will have clearly articulated his or her vision for success and those on the team will understand their discrete role in contributing to that success. Further, the team members will understand what the military calls the "commander's intent." This allows team members to execute tasks in the absence of specific guidance or when time is critical and the decision maker is not immediately available. They are working on "all cylinders" and it shows. They have achieved synergy—like a high performance race car—everything is working, doing its job, so that the machine can perform at its ultimate potential. A beautiful thing!

7. Communication

It has been said that the greatest illusion about communication is that *it has taken place*. With multiple team members involved, communication, in all its forms, can become delicate, if not dangerous. Synergy is more easily achieved with personal, face to face interaction, and displayed high levels of trust. With trust, comes risk. We have to be willing to assume the risk of communication failure to ever hope to achieve communication success.

So much of our ability to create synergy within a team boils down to communication. Demonstrating openness, respect, opportunities to learn, active listening skills and our ability as project managers to follow through on those conversations are fundamental to create and sustain team synergy. Working with group ideas, checking on team members' needs, planning for difficult discussions, demonstrating consistency and more will help to model the type of synergistic behavior that is desired from all members of the team.

8. Risk

As a project manager, while we assume much of the risk; it needs to be shared as well. Shared risk is a hallmark of high performance teams. Leaving the project manager to "twist in the wind" serves no useful purpose and "taking one for the team" is over-rated, at best. The most successful project mangers, like the most successful coaches, create an environment where people are mutually supportive, held accountable for their actions and share the risk of failure.

The upside, of course, is that shared risk and shared failure softens the blow of defeat. The downside is that it may be difficult to identify the reasons for the failure. The first place to look should be the design and functionality of the team itself and to examine if all the risk was with one person.

9. Procurement

Project managers may be responsible to secure goods and services to support the delivery of the product or service required of the team. The successful project manager will consider all aspects of these procurement activities and decisions before taking action. Again, synergy and unity of effort come into play.

When procurement activities are aligned, coordinated and organized, the probability for success increases. This alignment is important not only in the timing of these actions, but in the specific relationships between and among the service or product providers. Here, the project manager must acquaint him/herself with the prospective providers, examine their unique abilities to meet their needs and seek to take advantage of their ability to compliment one another and the team itself. Synergy within the procurement activity will result in quicker starts, shorter lag time and reduced costs over time.

"A lot of what we will do is get our arms around what we have.
Look for ways to create synergy and then get everybody
driving down the road in the same direction.."
– DON SNYDER

IX.
Conclusion

"To succeed, jump as quickly at opportunities
as you do at conclusions."
– BENJAMIN FRANKLIN

Only our time and experience will tell if we have been at all successful, that is to say, helpful in identifying and clarifying the concepts of conflict in relation to our work as project managers.

Our writing has proven valuable to both of us as authors, managers of resources and leaders of people. We sincerely hope that that value reaches everyone as well.

Both of us felt at the outset of this endeavor, and continue to feel strongly today, that only a thorough dissection of the elements of conflict – its good, bad and sometime ugly sides – will help to understand its origins, its use and its meaning in our professional and personal lives. Perhaps no other form of management lends itself more readily to the study of humans in conflict than does project management. Ambitious, if not aggressive timelines, limited resources, stringent deliverables and extraordinary demands on quality present the perfect prescription for conflict. And just when the project manager has no spare time with which to effectively deal with conflict, is generally the exact moment when it requires his or her undivided attention. Our book has been an attempt to address that moment and arm the reader with the tools, skills and awareness to adapt to, overcome and ultimately control that conflict.

As we reviewed the elements of F.A.C.T.S. (Fear, Anger, Control, Trust and Synergy) within the context of life as a project or program manager or project team member, we discovered something we ourselves had not really expected. We found that the rubric of the project—with its hard deadlines and countless other constraints—provides a microcosm of life in the workplace. Everything is accelerated—the highs are higher because they result in comparative "instant" gratification. The lows are lower because recovery time is essentially nil. Relationships are forged in an almost "combat-like" setting and as such, can either turn sour fast and end badly or be the foundation of a lifelong comradeship. The many and diverse stakeholders that are constantly cared for and nurtured by the team and its leader will form a lasting impression of the value of project management, based mostly on the outcome and partly on the process we follow.

The skills of the project manager in terms of planning, organizing, motivating, problem solving, supervising, delegating, innovating and cooperating along with his or her resourcefulness, creativity, initiative and judgment will be forever imprinted on the minds of everyone connected with that project. That's a lot of pressure to handle and it normally comes with no "how to" book to help guide the way. This pressure is the playground for unproductive and debilitating conflict.

It's not just important—it is ESSENTIAL that each of us involved in project management understand how conflict works, where it hides and how to put it to good use. It's a fact of life in this environment, and avoiding it is clearly not the solution. We can only fix what we understand. We hope that we have helped to uncover that unknown.

Dave Gerber
Dave Maurer
January 2008

More on leadership from the authors...

As we end this discussion on conflict in project management, it seems fitting to consider the driving nature of the high performing leader; the one who most effectively handles conflict and the myriad other distractions and impediments to superior performance. In a world of bland, dispassionate and sometimes cold leadership, these leaders are exhilarated, intense and full of vigor...we believe they are "On Fire."

People can see it in their eyes, their approach and their actions. They come to work with a spark that sets the tone for the day or the project and we wonder, "...where do they get that energy?" Maybe they love their work or the people on their team. We think it's that and much more. It's a mind set. It's a willingness to try new things, to risk more often and to learn to trust our own informed judgment and experiences. Good leaders have that spark – GREAT leaders ignite the flame in their colleagues, subordinates, superiors and everyone around them. An "On Fire" leader is never alone - an "On Fire" leader gains a following and lights the way to success!

Take YOUR leadership to the next level. Visit **www.onfireleadership.com** for more information!

X.
About the Authors

*"Great teamwork is the only way we create
breakthroughs to define our careers."*
— PAT RILEY

As President of Synergy Development and Training, **Dave Gerber** has dedicated himself to helping individuals, businesses, non-profits and government agencies. He helps these organizations use conflict and leadership development opportunities to build stronger and healthier structures, enhance productivity, increase revenue and reduce risk.

Innovative, dynamic, humorous, and passionate are just a few words that are used to describe Dave Gerber's impact as a speaker. Blending his engaging personality with actionable substance, he does more than generate interest; he stirs people to action. Dave employs humor, interaction, multi-media presentations, and a multitude of communication styles to quickly connect with any audience, disarm resistance and share his message. Individuals walk away not merely moved, but changed, energized and optimistic.

Dave is known as the "King of Conflict" for his powerful keynote addresses on conflict management. This topic, however, is only one among many in his repertoire. He is the only presenter in the world to use a moving sand film, "Synergy," as an introduction and launching point to illustrate the themes of the presentation. This always resonates as a topic of conversation long after this powerful presentation. In carefully honed words and persuasive images, Dave reveals a formula for excellence that begins with focused and effective action targeted at the right people joined in a common purpose.

Dave Gerber has always harbored a passion to help people improve their professional and personal lives and to assist organizations in fulfilling its mission. This desire to inspire excellence is supported by his strong educational background and unmatched experience.

He received his undergraduate degree in Sociology from Ithaca College, a Master's degree in Education from Saint Joseph's University in Philadelphia, and a Senior Executive Leadership Certificate from Georgetown University. His extensive hours of training in conflict management and alternative dispute resolution add to his already impressive credentials and reputation. Dave has acquired a Master Certificate in Business Analysis and a Master Certificate in Human Resources from Villanova, as well. Using training, coaching, speaking and writing opportunities, Dave continues to make a significant positive impact on everything he touches.

Dave Maurer is a board member of the Washington D.C. Chapter of the Project Management Institute and a Vice President with Axiom Resource Management, Inc., a professional consulting firm providing program management, operational support, accessibility, management training, distance learning, and IT solutions to dozens of private, state and federal agencies spanning several states. Their principal clients include the Departments of Defense, Education, Housing and Urban Development, Justice, Labor, Transportation, Treasury and Veterans Affairs, the Federal Aviation Administration, the Centers for Disease Control and Prevention, the IRS and NASA. Axiom also serves within the Office of the U.S. Army Surgeon General and the National Institutes of Health.

Dave's work ranges from process improvement, reengineering, training, and administration and management to implementing sweeping changes in component structure and composition. He has delivered numerous presentations on Leadership, Ethics, Negotiation Skills and Project

Management to audiences that include the World Bank, the Central Intelligence Agency, the Federal Bureau of Investigation, the Project Management Institute, the United States Marine Corps, The United States Air Force, the United States Military Academy at West Point, the State Department Federal Credit Union, and the National Summit on Project Excellence in Government, among others. He has also guest lectured for the University of Maryland's Smith School of Business MBA Program.

Dave serves on the Board of Directors for the Washington D.C. Chapter of the Project Management Institute; the largest chapter in the world with nearly 8,000 members. He earned his certification as a Project Management Professional (PMP) in 2003.

Prior to entering the private sector, Dave served in the U.S. Army for nearly 22 years, retiring in 1999 as a lieutenant colonel. He served in numerous command and staff positions, most notably as the Deputy Adjutant General for the U.S. Army in Southern Europe, Executive Assistant to the Director for Manpower and Personnel, Office of the Chairman of the Joint Chiefs of Staff at the Pentagon, and as the 72nd Adjutant General at the United States Military Academy at West Point.

Dave also serves on the Board of Advisors of the George Washington Chapter of the Association of the United States Army, and has been a volunteer Hospice Counselor and a mentor for Seton Hall University business students. He previously served on the Board of Directors for the USO of Metropolitan New York City, the Chamber of Commerce for the city of Butte, Montana, and as a director or president of several Rotary and Kiwanis service clubs.

Dave earned his Masters Degree from Central Michigan University in management and his Bachelors Degree in economics from Seton Hall University in New Jersey. He is a graduate of the Army's Command and General Staff College and several military courses of study.

Suggested Resources

www.synergydt.com
www.davegerber.info
www.kingorqueenpm.com
www.kingorqueenbooks.com
www.useconflict.com
www.davegerberproducts.com
www.onfireleadership.com
www.davegerberbooks.com
www.axiom-rm.com

XI.
Works Cited/Consulted

In Print:

Fischer, Robert, William Ury, and Patton, Bruce, *Getting to Yes: Negotiating Agreement without Giving In*, Penguin Group, New York, 1981.

Gerber, Dave, *Use Conflict: Advance Your Winning Life*, Timeless Publishing, Virginia, 2006.

Gerber, Dave and Leech, Pamela, *Life without Conflict: Introduction to a Winning Life*, Timeless Publishing, Virginia, 2006.

New World Dictionary of the American Language, 2nd edition, "Fear," Simon and Schuster, Tree of Knowledge, New York, 1984.

Online:

International Institute for Restorative Practices, "What is Restorative Practices," *International Institute for Restorative Practices*, n.d., <http://www.restorativepractices.org/library/whatisrp.html>, (July 26, 2006).

McManamy, John, "Anger and Depression in Bipolar Disorder," *McMan's Depression and Bipolar Web*, n.d., <http://www.mcmanweb.com/anger.htm> (July 26, 2006).

Messina, James J., Ph.D., "Growing Down: Tools for Healing the Inner Child Letting Go of Shame and Guilt," Coping.org, n.d., <http://www.coping.org/innerhealing/shame.htm> 2006.

Panic-attacks.co.uk, "Part 5: The Brain and Panic Attacks: Emotional Hijacking," *The Panic Attack Prevention Program*, 2001-2006, <http://www.panic-attacks.co.uk/panic_attacks_5.htm /> July 26, 2006.

Rotter, Julian, "The Social Learning Theory of Julian B. Rotter," California State University, Fullerton Department of Psychology, September 11, 2005, <http://psych.fullerton.edu/jmearns/rotter.htm> (July 26, 2006).

"The Guide to the Project Management Body of Knowledge" 3rd Edition, (C) 2004 Project Management Institute.

Wordreference.com, "Conflict," *Wordreference.com*, 2003, <http://www.wordreference.com/definition/conflict/> (July 26, 2006).

Appendix:
Synergy Planning Guide

By using this the following form to prepare for a negotiation, difficult conversation or conflict, we can be more prepared to disarm the conflict and move to individual and mutual needs.

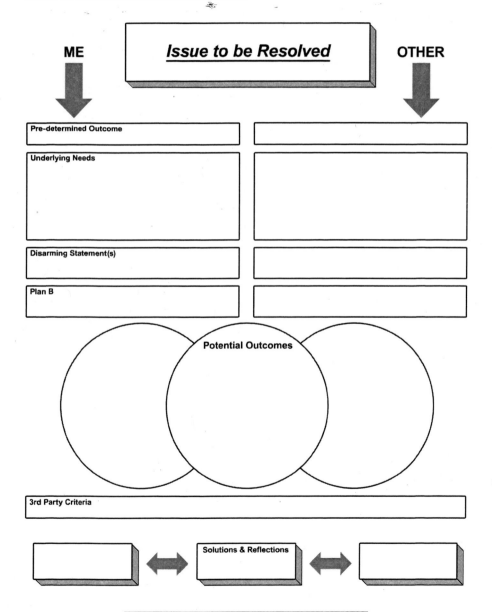

ME

OTHER

Issue to be Resolved

Pre-determined Outcome

Underlying Needs

Disarming Statement(s)

Plan B

Potential Outcomes

3rd Party Criteria

Solutions & Reflections